Ninety percent of the passengers on your flight will be casualties of air travel. Are you going to be one of them?

Are you one of the nine out of ten passengers who will experience some kind of discomfort during flight or after landing—discomfort caused by excessive radiation, pesticide sprays, lack of humidity, or oxygen deprivation?

Did you know passengers in tourist class receive 50% less fresh air than inmates in federal prisons?

But you are not doomed to walk off a plane with swollen feet, a sinus headache, a lower than normal level of clarity, a backache, or the bug you caught from breathing recycled air filled with germs—not if you follow the easy directions in JET SMARTER.

With hundreds of tips proven effective to make flying less tramatic, less hazardous, and a lot more enjoyable, JET SMARTER can help eliminate the downside of jet travel forever.

How much will your flight rob you of health, energy, and a clear head? It's your choice.

Diana Fairechild

JET SMART *Reviews*

—General Electric Corporate Newsletter

"JET SMART is required reading for anyone interested in better, smarter air travel—the perfect gift for anyone who flies, and a useful tool for business travelers."

—Meeting News

"Fairechild tells you how to minimize the emotionally draining, irritability-causing, and even life-threatening effects of flying."

—Mimi Weisbord, Healthy Home & Workplace

"I love this book. It is so intelligent, full of good research, good writing, funny, and spiritual all at the same time."

—Forbes

"A hot-selling treatise on jetlag."

—Environ Magazine

"*Jet Smart* dropped a bomb in Washington, and the Environmental Protection Agency and Department of Transportation changed policy."

—Noel Brown, MD, United Nations Environment Director

"I will distribute *Jet Smart* to my frequent flying colleagues."

—Joan Duncan Oliver, US Air In-flight Magazine

"Diana Fairechild says, 'change of environment, change of climate and environmental stress en route all contribute to the severity of jetlag.'"

—Karin Winegar, Conde Nast Traveler

"Fairechild says on certain international flights, attendants are required to empty half a dozen cans of pesticide into the passengers' air supply."

—The Direct Issue

"Fairechild's book is a result of her own experience with flight-induced maladies. This book is a blessing in disguise because she has had to suffer a long recovery in order to offer sound advice to readers."

—The National Law Journal

"Ms. Fairechild, an activist in the movement to clean up the skies, deals decisively with such thorny (and, in many cases, previously undisclosed) in-flight environmental issues as pesticide spraying (which she calls 'killer mists'), toxic chemicals, secondhand smoke, radiation, ozone, bad air, noise, and electromagnetic pulses."

—Arthur Spiegelman, Reuters News Service

"The self-help book has reached new heights thanks to a grounded airline stewardess who single-handedly has written, published and promoted the first book on how to survive the discomforts of flying. And she also acted as a private detective quite a few times, thinking up reasons to sneak into the cockpit to see if the pilots had reduced the airflow for passengers while maintaining it for themselves. Reducing the airflow for passengers by a third is part of what Fairechild called 'the budget monster.'"

—Carol Lively, American College of Nuclear Physicians

"I suggest those of you who take long trips order a copy of JET SMART so that you will arrive healthy and relaxed."

—Barbara Gillam, Glamour

"Fairechild gives some sensible everyday advice that only an insider could know."

—Chicago Tribune

"How can you beat jetlag and increase your in-flight comfort? Take the advice of Diana Fairechild."

—International Airline Passengers Association
"We've read it and we love it."

—Georgia Nielsen, Air Reporter

"With a sense of humor she skillfully weaves into the prose, Fairechild offers a wide range of ideas for veteran crew as well as for the infrequent flyer."

—Coleman Andrews, Los Angeles Times

"She spices up her book with no-nonsense insider's asides that are often simply fascinating."

—Aloha Magazine

"Everything from preflight preparation to postflight acclimatization and all the little traumas in between."

—*Alan Isbell, Trade Winds*

"Diana Fairechild lays claim to the distinction of being the first airline employee to blow the whistle on the airline industry for health hazards to which it has routinely subjected passengers and crew."

—*USA Today*

"'Ask the pilot for *full utilization of air* if you have difficulty breathing or thinking. It could mean you're not getting enough air,' says Diana Fairechild."

—*Bill Kaufman, Newsday*

"A checklist for passengers."

—*Whole Earth Review*

"An enlightening, useful reference book."

—*Orange County Register*

"Fairechild's subject matter is how to combat the indignities and discomforts of air travel."

—*Journal of the Association of Interpreters*

"A remarkable discussion on defeating jetlag that includes medical, philosophical and holistic advice."

JET SMARTER
The Air Traveler's R$_X$

by
DIANA FAIRECHILD

FLYANA RHYME

JET SMARTER

Published by FLYANA RHYME
PO Box 248 · Anahola, Hawaii 96703 · USA

Phone 808/ 828-1919
Ordering line 800/ 524-8477
Orders from abroad 808/ 639-9900
E-mail diana@flyana.com
Internet www.flyana.com

The sole intent of the author and publisher is to offer information of a general nature. Should you choose to use this information, you are prescribing for yourself and the author and publisher assume no responsibility.

Front cover Ben Maiden
Author photo Ohana
Drawings Bart Goldman
Editorial assistants Jackie Levy, Dave Sanford, Brent MacKinnon, Jim Panos

Library of Congress LC: 99-94854
1. Travel—Health 2. Jetlag

ISBN: 1-892997-49-5

Kauai, Hawaii

Also by Diana Fairechild

JET SMART
Over 200 tips for beating jetlag

NONI
Aspirin of the Ancients

OFFICE YOGA
A quickie guide to staying balanced
and fit in the work environment

"HEALTHY FLYING" website

Table of Contents

*Familiarize yourself with jetlag—the
Laggin' Dragon. This is the first step
toward taming the beast.*

*Jetlag is compounded by the issues of
microbial infection, toxic sprays, aircraft blow-
outs six miles high, and cancer-causing
radiation. What can you do?*

Stalking the Dragon (*continued*)

Acknowledgements

JET SMARTER evolved like one of those big picture puzzles—piece by tiny piece. Each person listed on this page offered a unique, precious piece to the puzzle. Deep appreciation to the following friends for their help and support. Thank you.

Phyllis Abbott, Remy Agpaoa, Paula Akana, Dick Algire, Chris Altemeier, Nina Anderson, Coleman Andrews, Robert J. Barish Ph.D, Robert O. Becker M.D., Art Bell, Ed Belway, Susan Boatright, John Bogert, Lori Brewington, Jane Brody, Noel Brown M.D., John Campbell, JoAnn Carroll, Chin-Ning Cheu, Jonathan Collin M.D., Wanda Cook, Chris Cooke, April Courture, Ron Dalquist, Sandy Dennison, Kathleen Donnely, Frances Dougherty, Dan Dryke, John Duffy, Linda Edison, Charlie Elias, Pearl Elias, Muriel Eloy, Jill Engledow, Linda A. Evans, David Every, George Ewing M.D., David Fisher, Bob

Franklin, Barbara Gillam, Randy Gingras, Linda Glas, Jim Gordon, Ruby Grace, Jasbir Grewal, Alaya Hannan, Brenda Harrison, Jerry Herbert, John Hills, Cheryl Holmes, Fred Hornbruch, Charles Horner, Nancy Humphreys, Renee Ingram, Alan Isbell, Brian Janssen, Bea Jauncey, Abe Jones, Jonny Johnson, Bill Kaufman, Michael Kanouf, Annette Kaohelaulii, Dan Karlinsky, Gladys Kelley, Ed Kennedy, Jonathan Kirsch, B.J. Kirwan, Chris Koller, Kurt Koller, Dorothy Korn, Lutz Kroth, Gary Kubota, R.J. Lafond, John Lazzaro, Ben Maiden, Esther Manning, Mary Ellen Mark, Vincent Mark M.D., Carol McCullough, John McManus, James Miller M.D., Kirstin Miller, Dr. Lucy Miller, Gareth Morrell, Manfred Mroczowski, Valerie Muroki, Patt Narrowe, Dennis Nelson, Fred Nott, Ohana, Joan Duncan Oliver, Diane Oosterveen, Diane Orenstein, Clyde Ota, Jim Panos, Cindy Paulos, Paris Permeter, Dee Pollock, Dan Poynter, Salli Rasberry, Rhonda Richards, Andrew Rogers, Roy Rowan, Joseph Ryan, Dave Sanford, Peter Sanford, Vince Savarese, Ann Schneider, Suda Scott, Jeff Segawa, Robbie Sherson, Heidi Schultz, Rona Smith, Arthur Spiegelman, Maggie Stanford, Evelyn Staus, Chuck Tipple, Nan Tipple, Marty Tolchin, Tony Verga, Bertil Werjefelt, Dove White, Leslie Wilkox, Paul Wood, Jon Woodhouse, Frank Yap, Mary Zanakis.

Foreword
George Ewing, M.D.

In JET SMARTER, Diana Fairechild exposes, with great depth and poetic detail, the hazards of air travel. When her first book JET SMART came out, I knew her writing would help to protect thousands of people all over the world.

The information is of vital importance because so many people travel and so many people get sick when they travel. This reason, among many others, makes it a pleasure for me to write a foreword for JET SMARTER.

Diana's previous long career as an airline flight attendant provided her with vast knowledge and painful personal experience of the problems affecting airline passengers. Through her own process of successfully coping with chemical sensitivities, she is well equipped to offer strategies for surviving the dangers we face in the enclosed, pressurized area of an airplane cabin.

Air in a pressurized cabin is recirculated continually. This same air circulates bacteria and viruses, as well as volatile odors from substances such as perfumes, lotions, and fabrics.

Although most airline passengers can manage to tolerate the closed, controlled environment of an airplane, many individuals will knowingly, or unknowingly, react to unsuspected volatile chemicals. This includes residuals of chemicals used to clean interiors as well as to eradicate and prevent insect infestations.

To the susceptible individual, symptoms can be neurological with fatigue, tension headache, nasal and respiratory congestion, and depression. Short infrequent exposures will produce minimal problems, but long flights, four to five hours or longer, may cause significant symptoms.

A cabin, pressurized to an elevation of 8,000 feet, provides a comparable oxygen level that would be present at any 8,000-foot elevation. This amount of available oxygen may be less than people who live at lower altitudes are used to.

Oxygen in tissues is essential to the body, detoxifying it and reducing symptoms relative to chemical exposures. Particularly sensitive individuals who have marked reactions to volatile chemicals may need to have additional oxygen provided on long trips.

This is essential, since oxygen is necessary for the brain and for the detoxification systems of the body to work properly.

Diana Fairechild has made it possible for the airline passenger to avoid most air travel maladies, by doing a remarkable job of turning her disability into an instrument of value for the traveling public.

Her book, JET SMARTER, goes beyond offering passengers ways to deal with the toxic airplane environment. It offers us hope that if enough of us learn about the hazards of air travel, the airline industry will be forced to resolve these problems.

GEORGE EWING, M.D.
Honolulu, Hawaii

Why flying is hazardous to your health

Flying is risky—risky beyond terrorists' bombs and airplane crashes. Your seat at 35,000 feet is a vortex of sky-high stress. Cancer-causing radiation and toxic pesticide in the oxygen-deprived environment of an airplane cabin damage the health of every passenger on board.

This book gives you the tools to safeguard your health when you fly. Alongside each health risk, strategies are offered to assist you in taking all necessary steps to prevent it or, when necessary, remedy its hazardous effects.

How many people do you suppose get sick every year from flying? Everybody on board (except pilots in the cockpit) is forced to breathe the recycled cabin air—air which often carries contagious diseases. According to the surveys conducted at my website, "Healthy Flying," nine out of every ten passengers becomes ill after flying.

Unfortunately for passengers, and probably to the airlines' relief, the link between air travel and illness is not always immediately obvious because contagious diseases have an incubation period before symptoms manifest.

Airline passengers generally get sick after they land. Since passengers disperse after landing, it's tricky to connect their illnesses with specific flights. The airlines bank on this lack of a clear connection between air travel and illness.

It is ironic that people are preoccupied with the possibility of plane crashes—events that are relatively rare—since for every one person who dies in a plane crash, half a million will probably become ill after flying.

Of course, getting sick after you reach your destination is not the same as dying to get there! But the huge number of people who are getting sick affects us all. Anyone could become infected by an air traveler who passes a flu bug to his child, who passes it to yours, and then to you.

Another potentially serious environmental hazard for airline passengers is toxic chemical poisoning. I should know. I flew 10 million miles as an international flight attendant until I was medically grounded—chemically poisoned from the pesticides, jet fuel fumes, and tobacco smoke in my workplace.

This unequivocal determination was made by George Ewing, M.D., allergist and immunologist at Straub Hospital and Clinic in Honolulu, and supported by three other physicians who also specialize in toxic chemical poisoning.

A toxin is defined as "a substance which can cause death, disease, behavioral abnormalities, cancer, genetic mutations, physiological or reproductive malfunctions or physical deformities in any organism or its offspring. . ."*

Today, air travel is synonymous with exposure to toxic substances.

All in all, flying is hardly "friendly" and certainly not the glamorous event of yesteryear. But the fanciful myth of glamour still persists, and perpetuating this glamour myth is a primary objective of airline advertising.

Flying used to be something that people enjoyed, but airline glamour officially died with Deregulation in 1978. I witnessed the change. More than the rolls became stale. The air became stale, too, as cutting corners, including the oxygen supply, became an obsessive preoccupation of airline management.

The changes in my workplace inspired me to start writing JET SMART in 1978. Eight years later, my

*The International Joint Commission (IJC), 8/12/98, *Rachel's Environment & Health Weekly* #611, <erf@rachel.org>.

bout with "toxic chemical poisoning" refined my focus on environmental health.

JET SMART was published in 1992, a year when I was too ill to go on a book tour. Nevertheless, the book got a lot of press—starting in Hawaii, where I live, as tourists took copies home with them.

The information in JET SMART is so important that people pass it along through a passionate wireless more potent than any New York publicist.

Barely thirteen months after JET SMART was first published, a *USA Today* feature in the "Business Section" called it "an underground hit." To date, over 300 media references and articles have appeared. Some are excerpted for you at the front of this edition.

I'm thrilled that this coverage has increased public awareness about aviation health. There have been a number of changes in the industry, and I believe JET SMART and informed passengers have played a role.

One case in point: JET SMART originated the report that the air supply of pilots is separate from that of the passengers. The pilots I worked with always argued that they didn't have separate air. But, when I visited the cockpit to serve them drinks or meals, I knew the air was different—fresher, richer.

Later, when some flights became "no smoking," research surfaced in a newspaper article that supported what my senses had already clearly confirmed and my co-workers had so emphatically denied. The article revealed that passengers could be guaranteed tobacco-free air on no-smoking flights, even if their pilot smoked, because the cockpit always had separate air. (Please see the chapter "Smoking" for full details.)

Over the years, as my writing has become more visible, a number of pilots have tried to convince the media that I don't know what I'm talking about. A few of these encounters are documented for readers on my website page <www.flyana.com/full.html>.

After I stopped flying and JET SMART was published, all U.S. flights and many international flights became "no smoking." Smoking continues, however, on some international routes. Passengers and flight attendants still have to endure the toxic secondhand fumes. (See "Smoking.")

In 1994, 60,000 ill, non-smoking, active and former flight attendants, charging that cigarette smoke in their workplace caused lung cancer, filed a class action lawsuit against seven tobacco companies. The attorneys for the flight attendants requested copies of JET SMART and, happily, I sent them. In 1997, the case was settled. The flight attendants with lung diseases and other smoking-related ailments got nothing. Nothing! Not a cent! Not even a health care fund!

The lawyers for the flight attendants were awarded $46 million in fees, plus another $3 million in court costs. The tobacco companies won the right to administer their own $300 million medical research fund. In spite of this blatant justice-gone-amok, it is with some satisfaction that I now see many airlines advertising that their flights are "no smoking." Cleaner air is a selling point today—as it should be.

But you won't see airlines advertising they don't spray their planes with pesticide. JET SMART's disclosure about pesticides in airplanes started a world-wide investigation, and at least twenty countries have stopped the horrific practice of spraying pesticide on airline passengers. The EPA and DOT have changed their policies as well, making it illegal on U.S. carriers to spray pesticide while passengers are on board.

Still, tragically, more than a dozen countries continue to spray passengers with poison! Further, another half dozen now require—unbeknownst to passengers—an extremely toxic "residual" pesticide which is designed to have its fumes circulate all flight long. (See "Pesticide.")

This brings us to another hazard. Some individual airplanes make people sick—and there are no records kept. Daily, people blindly walk into these "sick airplanes." (See "Toxic Chemicals" and "Airline Policies.")

28

In one incident, three flight attendants were taken to the hospital after something in the cabin of their aircraft made them ill. Without notifying passengers, airline management called in three standby crew members from reserve, put them in that same aircraft, closed the door, and the flight left on time.

Sadly, except for the increase in no smoking flights, it is still business as usual for the airlines. Take the seats, for example. A first class seat today on a U.S. domestic flight is about the same size as an economy seat on a DC8 in the mid-sixties. And then there's the air—it gets more stale every year as the airlines recycle larger and larger percents.

Initially, I simply set out to disclose this kind of information to passengers so they would realize that the toxic environment in airplanes is partially responsible for their jetlag. However, JET SMART, as it turned out, however, set many waves in motion, and my allegation that the commercial jet cabin is highly toxic is now supported by many other researchers. Flight attendants who get ill now are able to point to their toxic workplace. Indeed, several class action lawsuits are pending—one for pesticides, one for oil fumes leaking into the aircraft's air conditioning system, and a third for hydraulic fluid fumes in the cabin air.

Awareness is growing, but some issues still need attention.

—**Recycled Air**: Airline pilots receive ten times more fresh air than the economy passengers do. What are the long-term effects of oxygen deprivation, and how does the recycled air in planes spread contagious diseases on a worldwide scale? Guidelines from the World Health Organization clearly point out that **the airlines have not been notifying passengers who were on flights where a TB carrier was on board.** WHO advises that boarding should be denied passengers who have infectious TB because "In-flight exposure to infectious tuberculosis has become a realistic airline possibility owing to the high prevalence of tuberculosis in some regions of the world."[1] (See "Air Quality.")

—**Air Rage**: Emotional jetlag is due, in part, to the combined stresses affecting airline passengers—specifically, the poor air, the toxic chemicals, crowded seating, and the alcohol—all in low air pressure. (See "Symptoms & Remedies" and "High Altitude.") At least one flight attendant who was hit over the head with a vodka bottle is suing the airline, her employer, for not protecting her.[2]

—**Alcohol and Altitude**: Alcohol's diuretic properties exacerbate jetlag. Why do the airlines keep pushing alcohol on all the beverage carts? The airlines should be carrying enough purified water instead, to

30

provide everyone an adequate supply of water to combat dehydration in the airplane's near-zero humidity. (See "Dehydration.")

—**Melatonin**: My negative prognosis for this drug is now substantiated by other researchers. In spite of all the hype, melatonin for jetlag can be very dangerous. (See "Sleep.")

—**Ambient Light**: You can perceive light even with your eyes closed though scientists didn't believe this until five years after JET SMART was printed. Fluorescent lights should be dimmed on long flights to help passengers adjust their circadian rhythms (See "Light Therapy.")

—**Pesticides**: Recent scientific studies prove that the immune systems of animals and humans worldwide have been weakened due to constant exposures to toxic chemicals.[3] The residual level of pesticide which recirculates in the jet cabin borders on overload for many passengers and can cause pneumonia, infections of all kinds, and tuberculosis.[4] Instead of being properly cleaned, airplanes are often sprayed with pesticide.[5] On some international routes, pesticides are still sprayed directly on passengers while their seatbelts are required to be fastened and the air-conditioning is turned off. (See "Pesticide.")

There are dozens of health hazards endemic to modern airline travel which were first brought to public attention in JET SMART, along with over 200 coping strategies—some now widely circulated by the press. Through interviews, the press has also played up my personal story, which was not included in JET SMART.

I served on Pan Am for 19 years, then two more years with United after they bought Pan Am's Pacific routes. When I got sick while working for United, the company denied my appeal for Workers' Compensation. Neither the company nor the flight attendants' union acknowledged that my workplace was toxic, leaving me to deal with my health and legal problems in whatever way I could.

"What you've had to go through has probably made you far tougher than you ever imagined you could be," a reader wrote to me.

It *is* a great blessing to know that others are being helped by what I had to go through. So....I write. I watch. I urge. I wait for change. I interact on the Internet.

On the "Healthy Flying" website, several surveys have been conducted. Excellent information comes from readers. For example, while only 10% of respondents are most frightened of "terrorists," 64% are most frightened of "catching a contagious disease."

Incredibly, the airlines still claim that safety is a priority. However, this is limited to crashes, showing an obvious blind spot considering the health concerns now uppermost in the minds of passengers.

Over 90% of respondents to another "Healthy Flying" survey maintain that they suffer from symptoms of jetlag. Interestingly, more than one third of the thousands of people surveyed claim that their mental symptoms are even worse than their physical symptoms. (See "Symptoms & Remedies.") Before JET SMART was published in 1992, mental distress from jetlag was not even considered a credible symptom.

The simple truth is that our most severe jetlag symptoms could be reduced or eliminated if the airlines provided us with the basics: adequate air, comfortable seats, and pure water.

Ironically, most of what is offered on the airplane beverage cart (coffee, tea, soft drinks, and alcohol) exacerbates jetlag. (See "Diet.") I advise passengers to drink a lot of water when they fly—and to even bring their own water. There is no way we can count on an adequate and safe on-board supply of water. (See "Dehydration.")

I also advise passengers to ask the pilot for more fresh air. (See "Air Quality.") At first, crews usually complied when a passenger requested "full utilization of air"—the airline insider term for less recirculated air and more fresh air. Recently, however, passengers tell me that crews tell them there isn't enough fuel on board to fly with more fresh air and that the flight won't be able to make it if the percentage of oxygen is increased.

One passenger wrote me that even after someone on his flight fainted, the crew still refused his request for more fresh air. He was simply and abruptly told, "No."

The airlines deny that their cutbacks in fresh air adversely affect the health of passengers. Further, they explain that even if they wanted more oxygen in their airplanes, it's not possible since the newer models of jets all have "a diminished fresh air capacity." This excuse, introduced by the airline industry, has been widely discussed in the press.[6]

But it is only a half-truth. Although the 777 design (a design requested by the airlines) can't provide as much fresh air to passengers as the 747, it is still a management decision to reduce—even more—the passengers' fresh air on every flight in order to save on fuel costs.

My hope is that now, armed with the information in JET SMARTER, the flying public will demand that the aviation industry change its attitude and, more importantly, its practices. On the facing, page you will find a suggested letter you can adapt to your views.

Perhaps if enough of us write our legislators and other people of influence, such as newspaper editors, it will bring about reform requiring the airlines to make passenger health a high priority.

---

address
date

Dear Legislator/Editor:

For too long, the cabin environment in airplanes has been neglected. Health has been compromised by economy, and passengers have no control over the condition of their in-flight environment.

Besides appealing to the airlines, which I do, I would like the air travel regulatory bodies to take more responsibility in this key area of air travel health and safety. There are several cabin environment concerns that deserve attention, and air quality is the best place to start. Please help us to awaken the conscience of the airlines on behalf of the air traveling public. Thank you.

Sincerely,

Paul & Penny Passenger

Another step passengers can take towards making changes is to join the Fair Air Coalition (page 393). We are an activist group of concerned passengers and health enthusiasts—growing in number.

Prior to founding the Fair Air Coalition in 1997, I sent copies of JET SMART to airline management at all the major carriers in the hope that they would see that safe flying is responsible flying, and this includes the health of crew and passengers.

No responses, yet.

When JET SMART was first published, I felt a great satisfaction—a fourteen-year writing commitment was completed. But this turned out to be one of many steps in a lifetime commitment. It actually began when I was hired as an international stewardess. That was the beginning of my research into the causes of jetlag. I came to believe that jetlag was caused by more than just a time zone shift, which is all that researchers and writers wrote about until JET SMART came out.

After JET SMART was published, readers began asking me questions. I write to them when I can, and included at the back of this edition are fourteen letters I wrote that were first published on the ABC News website in 1997.

Jetlag and air-travel health are very complex subjects. When I was working on the revised and updated edition of JET SMART, I realized that I was changing so many things that it was really a new book. This book is 400 pages; the original JET SMART was 192 pages.

Further, to "jet smart" implies that "smart" is an end which can be measured. But "smarter" goes farther, with an endless end and a continuing process of becoming better.

So I now present to you JET SMARTER. All in all, I've been writing this book for twenty-one years. I consider this my life's mission, and I try diligently— every day—to help improve conditions for airline passengers. I hope this new book will be of benefit to you, to your colleagues, and to your loved ones.

Here, the air smells fresh. I pray for fresh ideas to help you, dear reader, in your travels and in your life.

Thank you. Take care.

DIANA FAIRECHILD
KAUAI, HAWAII

To flight attendants world-wide—
now 300,000 working.

And to my aunt Dot.E,
without whose help I could not
have completed this work.

Meeting the Dragon

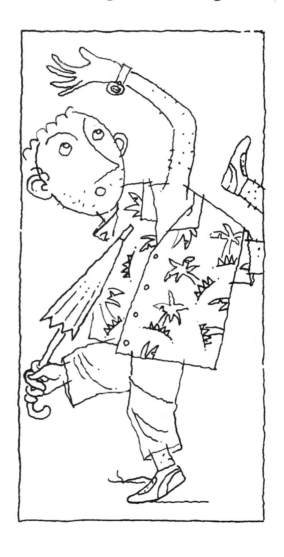

Air travel has become a beast. With sharp claws, the dragon rips us from the haven of the familiar. We call this feeling "jetlag." Each time we fly though the sky, we get pummeled by the wind of the dragon's wings and scorched by its breath of fire. We call this "the symptoms and discomforts of air travel." The dragon challenges us to new adventures in time and power. Become familiar with the Laggin' Dragon. This is the first step toward taming it.

Jetlag—What causes it?

> ➤ *When you first buckle up on board, set your watch to the local time at your destination.*

Jetlag can ruin a business trip, a honeymoon, or just about anything a traveler does in the days immediately after a long flight. Jetlag takes its toll on our health, our work, and our lifestyle. It can leave us stressed, ill, disoriented, or unable to function when we reach our destination.

Jetlag is caused by changes in the environment between departure and arrival zones, but also by the disruptive, toxic environment en route which severely reduces our fresh air supply and exposes us to significant amounts of germs, viruses, chemical vapors, pesticides, and radiation.

The combined effects of all the stresses bombarding air travelers causes jetlag. And the whole is greater than the sum of the parts, because the synergistic relationship of many stresses working together weakens the health and well-being of air travelers—sometimes subtly, sometimes severely.

Businesses are now taking notice because employees are becoming ill as a result of air travel. Among World Bank employees, for example, insurance claims of men who travel internationally are 80% higher than those who don't travel at all.[1]

Air travel affects the well-being of everyone on board, and especially so if you are pregnant, have a compromised immune system, a heart condition, lung disease, chemical sensitivities, or are elderly or very young.

Statistics now show that many passengers die after they fly.[2] A number of newborns have reportedly died a day or two after flying; researchers believe this is caused by the prolonged oxygen reduction in the airplane.[3]

Airlines do not let passengers know about the reduced oxygen. In fact, just the opposite is true—commercial jet travel is designed to hide the fact that you're hurtling through the upper atmosphere with diminished oxygen. A flight on a commercial jet is like an elaborate theatre of denial—the attendants in heels, the food, the booze, the movies, the shutting of window shades.

The illusion is catered to while actual needs are ignored. Passengers should be educated about the flying experience, but instead they are entertained, numbed, kidded, hoodwinked, and poisoned.

46

Passengers should be treated more as if they are going on a space shuttle flight and less as if they are on a bus. A plane is not a bus, not a movie theatre, not a cocktail lounge.

Fortunately, passengers can learn to protect themselves from the physical effects of flight, such as g-forces, changing time zones, dehydration, and especially the low air pressure, which adds to the reduction of oxygen.

Passengers can also learn to deal with the unnatural effects of flight caused by the airlines themselves—bad seats that can make a twelve-hour flight between Los Angeles and London feel like three years in a Roman galley; food and beverages that exacerbate the symptoms of jetlag; recirculating airborne diseases, such as the flu and tuberculosis; atmospheric radiation exceeding that of a chest x-ray on just an eight-hour flight; and pesticide sprayed on passengers as if they were vermin to be exterminated.

Jet cabins are among the most sickening environments in the world. Out of self-interest, airline companies have been suppressing this information, masking the problem as they continue to cause it. The airlines take no responsible measures to protect public health. Thus far, the government has stood aside.

Symptoms & Remedies

➤ *After flying, think twice before making commitments and important decisions.*

Over 90% of frequent flyers complain of physical and mental problems associated with long-distance air travel.

Of all the challenges air travelers face—rising air fares, terrorism threats, congested airports, flight delays, crowded planes, skimpy airline meals, aging fleets, air traffic tangles, inclement weather, and jetlag—it is jetlag that concerns people most, because they feel it long after their flights land.

Without understanding the mechanics of jet travel, an air traveler can suffer from jetlag for many days, even weeks.

There is little doubt as to the power of jetlag to cause increases in errors of judgment, accidents, and incapacitation on a global scale.[1] Jetlag is caused by environmental stress and environmental changes—and it is, literally, a roundtrip flight between cause and effect.

Our bodies are affected by jetlag

Jetlag can cause us to be clumsily out of step, even at those times when we are normally adept.

The sports page often blames jetlag for performances that are not up to par:

- In football, "Blame the jetlag and not the partying,"[2]

- In track, "Of course, there was jetlag,"[3]

- At the Olympics, "...loads of problems with jetlag,"[4]

- In chess, "Karpov complained of jetlag."[5]

Our minds are affected by jetlag

Jetlag can befuddle the mind—and priorities can easily get misplaced. It's like stepping off a merry-go-round only to discover you're not even at an amusement park! *Is that a brass ring you are grasping, or merely the key to another hotel room?*

In a deathbed confession, John Foster Dulles, diplomat and the U.S. Secretary of State in the fifties, blamed his own jetlag for the Suez Crisis. He said that heavy jetlag to and from Egypt prevented him from thinking clearly.[6]

Dulles was the first politician to admit that

jetlag had affected him. In 1954, Dulles' constant flying logged him over 100,000 air miles. Those miles took twice as long as they would today because jets hadn't been invented yet—showing us, too, that the physical and mental problems of jetlag predate the word "jetlag" itself and refer to all long distance air travel.

It is fitting that Dulles' name is so familiar to jetlagged travelers—at Washington-Dulles International Airport. As Dulles could fall victim to jetlag, so could you stumble during international business dealings and cost your company millions. Or harm your own career, perhaps. After flying, you might want to think twice before making decisions.

Our emotions are probably affected by jetlag

Like a nerve under a pulled wisdom tooth exposed to a rush of air, the unpleasant sensations we experience when we travel profoundly affect our tolerance, our discretion, and our moods.

Air rage, including brawls over armrests and assaults on crew members, are examples of emotional jetlag. Even Abu-Halima, when he was arrested for the World Trade Center bombing, pleaded innocent because he was suffering from jetlag. "He's disoriented and not in good shape," said Abu's attorney.[7]

Jetlag can cause our feelings to become more apparent, exposing our emotional underpinnings. Think twice before you speak. Be careful. Be kind.

Our very foundations may be shaken

Who among us has not wondered if we would survive a flight? Such thoughts lend themselves to spiritual reflection. But instead, many passengers act like the best cure for jetlag is to pretend it doesn't exist—getting plastered on alcohol, zonked on pills, or buzzed on sugar.

At-One-ness is another way to handle spiritual stress. Try prayer—instead of a whiskey—at high altitude next time. See where At-One-ness gets you.

➤ Remedies for you to choose from

The object of *Jet Smarter* is to enable passengers to become aware of the imbalances triggered by jet travel. Readers can then pick from the hundreds of remedies, choosing those that they find appropriate, convenient, and interesting.

Some remedies are preventive, such as picking a flight path that has less radiation when you are pregnant. Other remedies are more in the moment because some things cannot be avoided, such as the

Jetlag Symptoms (partial list)

Physical Jetlag:

body aches	irregular menstruation
constipation	loss of coordination
dry eyes/skin	loss of sexual passion
earache	low blood sugar
fatigue	modified drug reaction
headache	nervous tension
hemorrhoids	nose bleed
impaired vision	sore throat
insomnia	swollen feet
nausea	weakened immunity

Mental Jetlag:

confusion	poor concentration
indecisiveness	memory lapses

Emotional Jetlag:

anxiety	fear
depression	rage

Spiritual Jetlag:

at-numbness

dry airplane air, which dehydrates us. We all need to drink a lot of water before, during, and after air flight. This is most important for everybody who flies, so be sure to read "Dehydration," if you're skipping around.

Across the ten million miles I flew, many remedies crossed my flight path. A man once told me with all sincerity that, after every landing, he gulped down a whiskey miniature, and this insured that he never got jetlag. Another passenger, a woman from California, wore brown paper grocery bags around her shoes on every flight. She swore by them, and even gave me a couple to try. It seemed too silly, as if she had stepped into a bad practical joke.

All the tips offered here are personally verified. In my search to improve my own health when I was flying, I was always open to new ideas, especially on layovers around the world where I spent a lot of time pursuing health cures, doing yoga, going to seminars, and visiting spas. On the airplane, too, I was constantly on the lookout for new coping strategies. I experimented on myself and on colleagues and passengers who seemed open to new ideas.

While serving juice and hot towels, part of my brain was thinking about a greater service I could offer my passengers. On long-distance international flights, I saw how people were suffering, and I felt an urgent desire to help them to feel better.

Symptoms & Remedies: Strategies for self-defense

➤ After flying, think twice before making commitments and important decisions.

➤ Before you fly, assess your state of being. Even without diligent self-analysis, there are some obvious ways to prepare for flying, such as get lots of sleep prior to and after strenuous journeys and after night flights.

➤ The rest of this book offers you several hundred strategies for self-defense, specifically related to symptoms as they come up in the chapters. Symptoms are considered bodily signals. When we listen to these signals and make adjustments in our behavior, we start feeling better.

Time Zones—affecting bodily cycles

➤ *Spend time outdoors to synchronize your bodily cycles with local "climate cues."*

If we residents of Earth have a common language, it is *time*. We all agree about time. We have divided the Earth with twenty-four meridians, each corresponding to a one-hour segment in a day. If you look at a world map, you can see these twenty-four broad **zones** marking different **times**.

The physical, mental, and emotional symptoms we experience when we travel across time zones are definitely not psychological—they are *cycle logical*. Air travel disrupts all our internal cycles, which are synchronized to match our home time zone.

Cosmic events—such as sunrises and sunsets, moon phases, comets passing close by, solar eclipses, etc.—all influence our cycles, whether we're female or male, whether we're aware of them or not. Scientists have observed cyclic rhythms in humans, animals, plants, atoms, and even in stars.[1] Cyclic regularity is a basic underlying theme of life on Earth.

Cycles for all living things are as sure as the Sun rising every morning in the east and setting each evening in the west.

Yet, the realities of jet travel appear to invert the laws of nature. Jet travel can create a quirky kind of reality in which we see a sunrise set and a sunset rise. For example, when flying west in the morning at over 620 m.p.h., the aircraft flies away from the eastern horizon faster than the rotation of the earth, thus creating the oddity of the Sun's appearing to set in the east.

When we fly west in the evening, the Sun can appear to hover on the western horizon for hours, never fully setting—setting, rising, setting. On one flight, this phenomenon of a rising sunset caused much consternation to a certain Jewish passenger who was attempting to salute the setting Sun with his traditional prayer. The passenger rose and sat, rose and sat—painfully unable to reconcile the ritual he knew with the reality he saw.

Cacophonous conduct

Disorientation is a well-known symptom of jetlag. The reason is what takes place on a cellular level. Normally, all our bodily cycles work together harmoniously and precisely like the gears of a clock.

Each gear is of a different size. Each bodily cycle (temperature, sleep, hunger) is of different "sizes," too, in the sense that, after we fly, each bodily cycle takes a different amount of time to reset itself.

When we travel by jet, we fly across time zones faster than our cycles have time to adjust. All of our cycles are out of sync with the new time zone and out of sync with each other.

Body temperature gets out of sync with the new time zone and also out of sync with the sleep cycle.[2] Since our temperatures normally drop at night, this can result in feeling hot or irritable at night, being unable to sleep well at night, sleepiness at odd hours during the day, and also feeling cold during the day—all symptoms known to jet travelers.

Another way to think about this is to compare the body to a choral group. There are the sopranos, altos, tenors, and basses, normally all singing in harmony. After we cross time zones, though, tempos and tempers go off. If the sopranos start to sound shrill, sometimes even the conductor can't get them to stop. It's shocking to watch yourself go out of control like this—as if you suddenly saw the 13th hour on the clock.

Changing time zones actually forces every instrument in our bodily orchestra to change its tune—and the fleshly symphony can become a cacophony.

The conductor, the brain, tries to get all bodily cycles to work in harmony in the new time zone,[3] but what scientists call "rhythmic stability" prevents the cycles from quickly adapting. This protective reflex normally sustains us if we miss a night's sleep or a meal. Some time is required for the body to let go of its old habits, synchronized at home, and to be totally present and accounted for in the new time zone.

Once we let go of the old cycles, our internal clocks automatically reset in the new time zone. This happens even if we do nothing.

After flying, sleep and energy levels are usually restored to normal in a week, but some hormonal adjustments can take as long as two months. Even after being reset for the new time, hormones require more time to achieve the amplitude they had before leaving home.[4] This is why libidinal impulses and other grand hormonal events can make us feel out of sorts for longer than we'd like after flying.

Another way to become aware of jetlag is to keep track of body temperature. How does your temperature differ when you travel? And how long does it take for it to return to normal? If the reader is of the scientific sort, he or she may want to do the following body temperature experiment.

1) You need to establish your norm before

leaving home, taking readings with a thermometer for at least a week, twice daily, in the mornings and evenings. For most people, temperature cyclically peaks around 5 p.m. and dips around 5 a.m.

2) Watch how long your temperature remains out of sync after crossing time zones.[5] The average is around seven days.

3) When using an oral thermometer, be aware that anything recently in your mouth (even toothpaste)—and other circumstances such as infections, stress, and ovulation[6]—can all alter your temperature.

Flying east or west

Generally, passengers get more jetlag from flying east than from flying west. An exception would be flying west for ten hours and flying east for two hours because of the extra body burden of the toxic environment on board. For the most part, though, after eastbound travel, it's usually difficult to go to sleep at night because it's earlier than our normal bedtime.

When flying west, precisely because it's later than our normal bedtime at home, it's usually easy for us to fall asleep on local time.

A 1986 study on direction of flight found that recovery from jetlag took nine days after flying east[7] and only two to four days after flying west. The travelers were volunteers who flew back and forth between six time zones and were tested for body temperature, cognitive-motor skills, and fatigue.

The findings of a 1995 study of nineteen major league baseball teams agreed and went one step further; teams flying east, the study concluded, lose more games because flying east "diminishes strength and endurance."[8]

Flight attendants also prefer to fly west. Normally, flight attendants fly both east and west in the same pattern—for example, Los Angeles to London, then London to Los Angeles. But, in the early days of jets when I was flying with Pan Am, we also flew completely around the world—either eastbound or westbound. Even though the layovers in both directions were identical, the westbound route always went to senior personnel.

Oh, there was one more thing: westbound crews made more money because westbound flights took longer. London to Los Angeles (west) is actually several hours longer than Los Angeles to London (east). This is because eastbound flights (in the northern hemisphere) get a boost from atmospheric jet streams (similar to ocean currents). This adds to the speed of the plane without using extra fuel.

Flying west, bucking the jet streams, flights

are often turbulent and always slower.

Flying east is always a smoother ride, except in the Southern Hemisphere where the jet streams are reversed; Down Under, flying east is slower, longer, and more turbulent.

Flying east or west takes on a whole different quality when we cross the International Dateline in the middle of the Pacific Ocean. Westbound passengers miss a day. Eastbound, there's the peculiar illusion of living the same day twice. Though it's only an illusion, this calendar mix-up can take on a human significance when it comes to birthdays and holidays.

Jetlag and affairs of the heart

The heart rate takes about a week to beat the effects of jetlag. In the realm of subtle energies, this fact supports my theory that it is exceedingly difficult to sustain affairs of the heart over long distances, wherein one party travels across multiple time zones to rendezvous with a beloved. Did your heart skip a beat when you embraced your lover, or was it already tripped up? Are you falling in love or flailing in jetlag? We need to be able to trust our feelings. *Love requires wholeness of being which cannot be attained when a heart is divided against itself by jetlag.*

Passengers who suffer from cardiac weakness

may have a less romantic concern about heartbeats. According to one cardiologist, "People with heart disease require longer to recover from any stress, including jetlag. They shouldn't fly at night or travel more than three time zones without a rest stop."[9]

Passengers with weak hearts can use rest stops to recover, and three time zones is a good benchmark for taking it slower—unlike type-A business flyers who prefer non-stops and powering through stressful airplane rides. Passengers with heart conditions might also want to check with their airline to see if a defibrillator will be on board. Some airlines now carry them. If you experience irregular, uncoordinated heart contractions in flight, ring your call button or, better still, ask someone nearby to get a flight attendant—attendants may be busy and not answer the call button right away.

Heart patients and other passengers with medical conditions should check with their own physicians before flying. It is also wise to ask your doctor about your medications in relation to time zone shifts. Certain prescriptions, e.g., estrogen, need to be taken at regular intervals to be effective. Others must be ingested at specific times of the day, e.g., blood pressure medicine in the p.m. or diuretics in the a.m. Still others, such as insulin, require subtle adjustments of dosage when flying east or flying west.[10]

Time Zones: Symptoms you may experience

Confusion, digestive disorders, fatigue, impaired vision, insomnia, irregular elimination, irregular menstruation, low blood sugar, modified reaction to drugs, nervous tension, sleepiness, sleeplessness.

Time Zones: Strategies for self-defense

➤ When you first buckle up on board, set your watch to the local time at your arrival destination as a mental commitment to support the process of re-setting your biological cycles.

➤ Eating and sleeping on local time gives your body food triggers and social interaction ticklers that help the body's cycles to adapt.

➤ It is imperative to spend time outdoors every day, because the body needs the local light to synchronize itself with local "climate cues" (sunrise, noon light, moon light).

➤ Eastbound flights are faster and smoother, but westbound flights have less jetlag. After jetting west, it's easier to adjust our sleep rhythms. People who like to stay up late at night are the exception. They may find it easier to fly east.

➤ For the first couple of days after arrival, schedule work at a time when you are likely to have maximum energy:

• After jetting west, work in the morning.
• After jetting east, work in the late afternoon.

➤Remember that, after jetting, our internal clocks naturally reset themselves in their own time, but we can hasten progress or retard it.

➤Long distance travel:

• Modulates both the pulse and the yearnings of our hearts.
• Alters our brain waves and our capacity for comprehension.
• Skews digestion and balance.
• Tampers with reproduction and creativity.
• Stymies our sense of timing and the quality of our time.
• Affects our eyesight and insights.

North/South Flying —magnetic fields

> ➤ *Consider a near-equator rest stop—magnetic fields are milder so they don't affect us as much.*

Flying north or south over the equator disrupts our cycles differently—though no less forcefully—than flying east or west across time zones. I know of no other jetlag researcher who says this. Most other researchers base their findings on experiments in labs or isolated experiments in the air. I flew thousands of flights east and west and hundreds of roundtrips over the equator to South America and the South Pacific.

Flying east or west affects all our cycles and, most noticeably, the cycles of sleep and digestion. Flying north or south also affects sleep and digestion. In addition, it jolts our internal water reserves. There are many ramifications.

Down Under, water goes down the drain in a counterclockwise direction, just the opposite of the way it flows in the Northern Hemisphere.

If these forces can have such a dramatic effect on water in a sink or a bathtub, what is their effect on the water within the reservoirs of the human body?

Water gets agitated during transitions. In a bowl of water or in the bathtub, I can create waves with my hand. If I change the rhythm of my hand, the surrounding water becomes choppy for awhile before it settles into a new flow. Travelers also experience a period of "choppy water" after they fly over the equator. This delays the adjustment of their cycles.

Nature adjusts our bodily rhythms after flying over the equator in a two-step process:

> 1) The molecular structure of the cells needs to realign with the new magnetic field, then,
>
> 2) The cells can adopt the rhythms of the new time zone.

Compass confusion

Ships' compasses built in the Northern Hemisphere and operating in the Southern can take up to twenty years to be reset, using compensating magnets.[1]

Fluids, like crystals and magnets, orient toward the closest, strongest magnetic influence—either the North or South Pole. After crossing the equator, the human internal compass also needs to be reset.

Scientists have noted how shifts in geomagnetic fields can cause in us a lack of motor coordination that can result in increased accidents.[2] Water comprises over 90% of the liquid content of our blood, so, flying over the equator can reduce our ability to function in many ways: coordination (physically), memory (mentally), and gut feeling (emotionally).

Equator equipoise

Flying north and south also plunges travelers into a seasonal shift. We fly from spring to fall in a matter of hours. One day you are in Tokyo with pastel pink cherry blossoms on the trees. The next day, you're in Sydney with rust-colored leaves falling off the trees.

On a subtle energy level, there is a societal sense of optimism and renewal in springtime that seems absent in the fall.

North/South Flying: Symptoms you may experience

Disorientation, erratic behavior, fatigue, impaired coordination, impaired vision, irregular elimination, light-headedness, memory loss, modified reaction to drugs, nausea, weakened immunity, what we are attracted to, and what we attract to us.

North/South Flying: Strategies for self-defense

➤Take a hot bath after crossing the equator. Allow your internal fluids to attune to those in the surrounding water.

➤After landing, sleep with the crown of your head toward the North Pole or toward the South Pole. If you wish to tune into this subtle energy, try lying both ways on your bed and see if you can feel the difference. One direction has a stronger beat like a gentle pulsing entering the crown of the head and palpitating out the center of the feet. Which one should you choose? Both are good.

➤ Consider a near-equator rest stop. Here, magnetic fields are milder so they don't affect us as much.

Mega-Jetlag—an early grave

➤ *Review your mileage awards. Maybe you need a vacation to stay put and stay still.*

People who mega-jet for years come down with mega-jetlag. An example can be found in the story of the radio commentator Lowell Thomas, who was hospitalized in the sixties for a heart attack. He publicly stated that his heart condition was due to chronic jetlag.[1]

Mileage points add up

To determine if you might have mega-jetlag, consider if you're eligible for any of the airlines' frequent flyer bonus awards. The more bonus awards you accumulate, the more mega-jetlag you have.

Airline crews are all mega-jetlagged. Crew members accumulate as much as half a million miles a year, decade after decade. Pilots retire at age sixty. Pilots over age sixty have twice as many accidents as those in their fifties.[2]

Years of mega-jetlag can be likened to years of alcoholism. The high-altitude environment inhibits oxidation and is addictive.[3] As in tobacco, alcohol, and other addictions, there is a mechanism that throws off the system, confounding and confusing us. Like alcoholics, veteran sufferers of mega-jetlag develop ways to look good outwardly, affecting an illusion of normalcy while running the risk of deteriorating mind and organs in the long run.

Like all forms of addictive behavior, it is difficult for the addicted one to assess when he or she is acting out the addiction. Most frequent flyers don't stop long enough to notice that the cravings to get back on an airplane are actually withdrawal symptoms. I'd conservatively estimate that you have to stop flying for at least three months just to begin to touch base with these addictive cravings.

My own research reveals mega-jetlag has physical as well as emotional symptoms, including chronic fatigue, swollen lymph glands, weak kidneys, hyperactive adrenal glands, eye sensitivity, headaches, muscle twitching, temporary amnesia, susceptibility to staph infection—and the recurrent, addictive urge to jet away.

For short-term jetlag, there's a general rule, roughly one day of rest to recover for every time zone crossed. For mega-jetlag, there are no rules. No scientific studies have been done, to date, on the health and longevity of those who mega-jet.

Nevertheless, the British Airline Pilots Association reported "60% of premature pilot retirement is due to cardiovascular disease and the second most common cause was mental ill-health" including a high incidence of "behavioral peculiarities and alcoholism" epitomized by the expression that "the heart-case is not the real danger—the nut case is the killer."[4]

Tony O'Reilly, the high-society, jetsetting CEO of Weight Watchers and Waterford, commented on his jet commutes across the Atlantic with this distressing one-liner: "It is a formula for an early grave."[5]

Today, many business executives prefer video teleconferencing to continent hopping. Even Boeing, the aircraft manufacturer, boasts to have saved five million miles with video link-ups for their executives,[6] preferring video link-ups to flights in their own planes.

We've come a long way since 1903

A Boeing 747 airplane is longer from nose to tail than the entire distance covered by the Wright's first flight. Certainly Orville and Wilbur would jump with joy to see the latest 777. But, they would be astounded that millions of us are up in the air—without much fresh air to breathe.

Air, air everywhere, but not enough to breathe. The Wright brothers had no idea what they were getting us into.

Experience is a great teacher

On the positive side of mega-jetlag: when we are familiar with the in's and out's of a place, we experience less jetlag. Sitting at home, I may not be able to recall the subtle smells and sounds of a place, but every time I return there, it is familiar and I am more relaxed. I even sleep more soundly as the ambient noises don't trigger a need for me to awake and investigate.

Everything I've experienced, in this regard, is still readily available to me. I was away from Japan for ten years and when I returned, familiarity met me right at Narita Airport. The same happened in Hong Kong and in Paris—places I've been many times and stayed away from for long periods.

It's as if I have thought forms in those places, as easily donned as old favorite outfits, ready for me to step into any time I re-enter those zones.

Mega-Jetlag: Symptoms you may experience

Fatigue, headache, hemorrhoids, hypersensitivity, impaired vision, inability to concentrate, insomnia, irregular menstruation, memory loss, nervous tension, swollen lymph glands, weakened immunity.

Mega-Jetlag: Strategies for self-defense

➤Diminish mega-jetlag by taking care of yourself at each step of the way—on each leg of your journey. Then look back and see a healthier route taken and enjoyed.

➤Review your mileage accumulations. Maybe you need a vacation. Try not going anywhere for ninety days. Stay put. Stay still. Journey inside for a while and find those places in your inner world that need attention and restoration.

➤When we travel back to a familiar environment, its noises, smells, etc., may create an innate sense of security, translating into less jetlag.

➤If you haven't made a trip before, it helps to review it in detail with someone who has.

Stalking the Dragon

 *The dragon has many heads. One head is called "Radiation." Another is "Pesticide." When you slay one head, this horrible monster instantly pops out a new head. There is the head called "Ozone" and there's also "Toxic Chemicals." Egad! Be brave. For all the ways the beast can challenge you, there are more ways to defend yourself. Make the first move. Fly defensively. Be aware and take care. Use all challenges for personal strengthening.*

Compounding Jetlag

> ➤ *Examine all of the circumstances surrounding your flight, and do whatever you can to make it less stressful.*

The jet cabin environment is a place that is high in radiation, germs, and toxic chemicals and low in oxygen, pressure, and humidity.

When we jet, there are so many new stresses, it is difficult to assess what actually causes our symptoms. For example, do we feel out of sorts as a result of sleep deprivation? Was changing time zones the cause? That cough? Was it changing climates or the on-board ozone?

By the way, dry cough, when experienced by crew on polar flights, is commonly attributed to ozone. Impaired coordination is a symptom I track back to sleep deprivation, pesticides on the aircraft, and crossing the equator.

Each one of us has a different tolerance to these stresses determined by our medical history, age, accumulated jetlag, and even reasons for traveling. Every passenger has a unique experience with jetlag due to the multiple circumstances of air travel (see facing page) which we need to address so we can come to terms with our downtime.

Each person's resilience, combined with all the varying circumstances of air travel, determines the severity or mildness of his or her jetlag.

Here are some questions you may want to ask yourself when examining the circumstances of your flight. Armed with this information, you can better select your itinerary and, whenever possible, you can at least try to make informed choices and practice defensive flying.

- Is your flight a "red-eye" or a day flight ("Sleep")?

- Is there a solar flare on that day ("Radiation")?

- Does the passenger next to you cough incessantly ("Ozone", "Air Quality," and "Smoking")?

- Is a window or fuselage cracked ("Metal Fatigue")?

- Is the food of poor quality or just not what you're used to eating ("Diet")?

- Does the pilot offer fresh air, or is it recycled ("Air Quality" and "Airline Policies)?

- Have the on-board air filters been cleaned recently ("Airline Policies")?

- Was the airplane saturated with pesticide the night before your flight ("Pesticide")?

Circumstances of air travel

- Airline you fly
- Aircraft type
- Altitude of flight
- Class in which you are seated
- Direction of flight
- Duration of the flight
- Departure and arrival local times
- Fellow passengers
- Holes in the ozone layer
- News reports of recent crashes
- Percentage of recycled air
- Purpose of travel
- Seasons of embarkation/disembarkation
- Solar storm activity (radiation)
- Your accumulated jetlag
- Your age
- Your constitutional health
- Your fitness
- Your experience with jetlag
- Your worries
- What you ate yesterday

Aggravations aloft

The world record for the "fastest circling of the earth on commercial airlines" is held by David Springbett, who changed planes five times and flew the Concorde on one leg. It took David forty-eight hours, and the airfare cost $8,000; but he circled the globe in record time and won $10,000 by spending two days and nights in airplanes.[1]

People who circle the globe and then return home, or people who fly longitudinally, for example, from Boston to Bogota, still get jetlag even though they don't change time zones.

The reason? Jetlag is compounded by the on board environment. Flying in airplanes is stressful, risky, and fatiguing—not exactly a womb with a view.

Yes, jets are womb-like capsules which carry us almost in fetal position and then eject us under bright lights. But wombs sustain the well-being of babies, as opposed to the environment of commercial jets which drains the well-being of passengers.

Babies can't do anything about their situation. We, however, can. We can take care of ourselves and our loved ones.

Collectively we can call for reforms.

84

Air Quality–federal prisoners get better air

➤ *Ask the pilot for "full utilization of air."*

"I'm sick of getting sick on airplanes," said radio host Art Bell on his syndicated "Coast to Coast" show. Art explained, "I took a 757 down to Mazatlan, and I took a 757 back. And several days later, I got sick—really, really sick."

"Now I went to China," Art continued, "and I got sick. And I went to Paris, and I got sick. I am sick of getting sick on airplanes. Hacking. Coughing. Sneezing. Yesterday," Art shared conspiratorially with his one million listeners, "I was so out of it that when I was trying to fix something, I got superglue all over my hands. Then, like an idiot, I tried to pull the glue off with my teeth, and I put a finger in my mouth too soon—figuring it was already dry—and I glued my lip shut. And that's how sick I was. I completely screwed up there. You might be able to tell, I'm a little bit angry. So I have contacted somebody who knows about airplanes. I want to know about airplanes. I want the real scoop. Her name is Diana Fairechild. So we're going to ask her, why it is you get sick on airplanes and how you can prevent it?"[1]

Art Bell's opening statement made air quality on jets sound almost as dramatic as an aircraft exploding in the sky. Yes, the real air travel threat today is contagious diseases spread around the world by air travelers. Terrorism is not the biggest threat for flyers. Catching a contagious disease on board frightens passengers more than terrorism, according to my surveys on the Internet.

Incubation period

The incubation period for most contagious diseases means passengers are already home before trips to the Kleenex box start. For Art Bell, illness manifests several days after flying. For me, it has been a matter of hours, as the following incident illustrates.

On a night flight about six hours after takeoff, my throat swelled up, and within moments, five passengers complained to me of sore throats. "Orange juice, please. I have a sore throat," several passengers said to me practically in unison. Alarmed, I reported to the cockpit. The captain informed me, indeed, there was a severely ill child on board, though airlines normally refuse boarding to such passengers.

The captain had been personally petitioned and had made an exception. He told me this, then quickly put on his own oxygen mask. Pilots have pure oxygen on tap, in addition to 100% fresh air in the cockpit.

A nurse here in Hawaii told me that the emergency room at the hospital where she works treats tourists every day who have gotten sick on their flights. One 85-year-old man, she said, had pneumonia when he got off the plane. He flew here to visit his daughter, then spent his whole vacation in the hospital.

"Severe infections inevitably result from the prolonged recirculation of mixed viruses with 450 people in the confined space of airplane,"[2] explained Jacque Mar, M.D. in the *Journal of the American Medical Association.*

Especially during the colder months, frequent flyers complain nonstop of upper respiratory tract infections. The aircraft air filters do not remove germs. Anything smaller than an arthropod fragment (piece of a bug) is not likely to be caught, according to my research.

Further, many airlines neglect to regularly clean cabin air filters. Filters are often gummy with debris, much like old Notre Dame de Paris—crumbling in the face of this century's petrochemical pollution. On board, have a look for yourself. The air filters are high up in the galley in the ceiling panels.

Flying and the immune system

Although one week usually suffices to resynchronize the body after jetting, much more is required before we have the ability to respond to a "toxic challenge."[3] In other words, while it takes only a week to feel fairly normal after flying, it takes much longer for the immune system to recover.

Recycled Air: Strategies for self-defense

• Coat the inside of your nostrils with oil. This makes you less susceptible to catching a virus.

• Cover your nose and mouth with a water-saturated cotton handkerchief. This will help provide humidity for your lungs.

• Carry a disposable surgical mask in case someone on your flight has a hacking cough. You might present this individual with the mask, saying something like, *You will probably want to wear this to prevent the spread of germs.*

• Take echinacea and vitamin C to help your immune system fight off infections.

Fatigue from time zone changes and all the environmental factors on board synergistically make passengers more prone to contracting infections and less able to fight off viruses.

No fresh air when planes are on the ground

Documentation of contagious illness aboard commercial aircraft is rare because passengers disperse after landing. One incident, however, where an aircraft had a mechanical problem at a small airport in Alaska, clearly shows what can happen.

All the passengers were kept on board for four hours without air-conditioning before the flight was canceled. The only doctor in town reported that one person had the flu at the onset of the delay, and after three days, 72% of the passengers complained of cough, fever, fatigue, headache, and sore throats.[4]

A 1994 Harvard study[5] found that, although "in recent years, professional engineering societies have revised ventilation standards towards increasing fresh air, aircraft designers have actually reduced the fresh air." In addition, "carbon dioxide levels were substantially higher while aircraft were on the ground." This statement confirms what I said in JET SMART, that **reduced oxygen levels during runway taxis, during non-disembarking transit stops, and dur-**

**ing ground delays increase our risk of catching
dangerous infectious diseases.**

The 1998 guidelines issued by the World
Health Organization addressing the risk of tuberculosis transmission during air travel also support my
research referring to little or no ventilation during
delays on the ground.

After the airplane disengages from the um-
bilical to the airport air-conditioning system on "push
back," no fresh air is introduced on board until after
takeoff. Thus, on the ground, the possibility of spreading diseases is actually even more likely than in flight.

In 1986, the U.S. government Committee on
Airline Cabin Air Quality recommended that a regulation be established requiring removal of passengers
on the ground within 30 minutes of ventilation failure due to the likelihood of epidemic diseases.[6]

In spite of this, airlines still don't let people
off. In January 1999, a plane load of passengers was
held captive aboard a parked jet at Detroit airport for
eight hours. They are suing for "forced imprison-
ment."

Around the same time, I was on a flight that
had to go back to the gate because of a mechanical
problem. Everyone wanted to get off, but the ground
agents guarded the door and refused to let us go.
One person was crying, another was screaming.

What would you do if someone next to you or behind you had a hacking cough? I'd find another seat. If I couldn't find another seat, I'd tell the flight attendant, *I can't sit in that seat anymore because I'm afraid that passenger behind me may have TB.* You might have to stand the whole flight (or you might wrangle yourself into a first class seat).

Aircraft are contaminated

The effects of someone spreading a contagious disease are not confined to a flight. **Aircraft can be contaminated for many days. Respiratory droplets, spread by coughing, sneezing, even talking, accumulate on bulkhead panels, upholstered seats, and circulation systems.** Although the low relative humidity present in most aircraft during flight can be deadly for some bacteria, such conditions probably augment the viability of most viruses.[7]

On takeoff, spores wake up and jostle about like participants at a Brazilian Mardi Gras. They take to the air in microscopic clouds, then circulate among the passengers. Commercial jets are rarely disinfected. Like Brazilian playboys, they are constantly on the move. Planes stop in airports only long enough for teams of tidiers to race through their chores under the pressure of time constraints.

More recycled air, more diseases

The airlines have influenced the aircraft manufacturers to produce newer planes with less fresh air capacity. This is a regrettable circumstance of modern aviation that can only be changed by retrofitting the newer planes at their factories. In response to the accusation that these planes are actually harming passengers by causing more contagious diseases to spread, Boeing spokesperson Jack Gamble said, "If a guy with

---

How to know when cabin air is recycled

- You feel nauseated but there is no turbulence.
- Your lungs ache when you try to take a full, deep breath.
- You have a headache.
- The air seems stuffy.
- You notice you cannot easily concentrate on business work or even just reading.
- Your skin feels clammy.
- You feel like you might pass out.

92

the flu sits next to you and sneezes on you, you'll get sick. This has nothing to do with cabin ventilation."[8]

I disagree. **More fresh air, less chances of diseases spreading. More recycled air, more chances to catch something.**

The FAA's answer is to consider—not to mandate, but just consider—that future aircraft permit lower levels of carbon dioxide.[9]

Future transport? What about now? There are currently no rules protecting the air quality for passengers. The airlines systematically reduce the fresh air as a budget-cutting ploy, similar to the way a car owner turns off his air-conditioner to save on gas. In cars, of course, the air-conditioner is for comfort. In jets, it is for life support.[10]

To save money, the airlines mix at least 50% recycled air with fresh air pulled in from outside. As the ratio of recycled air is increased, the engines work less, less fuel is used, and the operating cost of the flight is reduced. Commercial jets rarely provide passengers with all the air *jets are capable of supplying*. On most jets, 747's for example, pilots flick off one of three available air packs* as standard operating procedure.

---

*An air pack is a function of the engine; outside, thin air is compacted to make the high altitude, unbreatheable air suitable for human consumption.

The pilots control the amount of fresh air the passengers get. Airline management, for the most part, requires pilots to routinely turn off one (of three) air packs, thus reducing the fresh airflow by one third. This saves approximately $80 an hour in jet fuel.

Rather than turn one off, many passengers might prefer that their captain pass the hat! The surcharge would only be about 20 cents per person per hour for a fully loaded 747.

On 767's and 777's, pilots recycle the passengers' air by turning ON the recirculation fans. It has the same effect—less fresh and more recycled air. The 767 instructions, according to one pilot,* are: "One or both recirculation fans, may be turned off for several minutes to refresh the air in the cabin."

This means that for several minutes, more fresh air will be introduced. *Several minutes? Who are they kidding?* Passengers need more than several minutes of fresh air! Try driving with the windows up in your car and the air conditioning on for only several minutes!

The pilot who sent me this information commented that both the manual and pilot verbal instruc-

*The pilot who sent this information to me said: "Here is something distributed by one airline to its crews that highlights its management's disregard for the passengers' comfort."

tions are presented in such a way that it is considered "normal" to turn OFF at least half the fresh air for passengers on every flight. Indeed, some airlines offer a bonus to captains who save the most fuel. One airline, he said, offers 3.5 hours of pay (about $500) each month to "the most fuel-efficient captain," but he wouldn't tell me which airline it was.

It is obvious that airlines which treat airplane air as a function of their bottom line do not realize that the more recycled air they introduce, the more vulnerable passengers are to the spread of diseases. Or they don't care.

Decreased oxygen in the central nervous system

Some doctors will go so far as to say that all of us riding in the cabins of commercial jets today suffer mild hypoxia, decreased oxygen in the central nervous system. Hypoxia symptoms are similar to those of mountain sickness: light-headedness, shallow breathing, fatigue, and inability to concentrate—the latter leading to multiple misadventures for the unknowing businessperson trying to prepare spreadsheets and expense reports.

If you feel spacey or have difficulty breathing, or you feel that the air is stuffy, you can ask for better air.

Symptoms such as clammy skin, impaired vision and unclear thinking can be tracked back to "hypoxia" (lack of oxygen to the brain).

Passengers can speak up and ask for the "air packs" to be turned on and the "recirculation fans" to be turned off, or they can request one of the many oxygen bottles kept on board.

How to get more oxygen on your flight

- Gently, kindly, ask you flight attendant (remember she or he is breathing the same air you are) to ask the pilot for "full utilization of air." Explain that you are having trouble breathing.

- Wait 15 minutes. If the fresh air has been increased, you'll find it easier to breathe. I find I also feel happier. You may even hear the air-conditioning get louder.

- If you don't feel better, ask for an oxygen bottle. There are about 20 portable bottles on each 747, and one will be brought to you at your seat. Sipping oxygen helps me, both en route and after landing.

Actually, it is crucial to tell an attendant if you experience difficulty breathing. The plane may have a slow decompression—a loss of pressure from a leaky door or a crack in the fuselage. (See "Metal Fatigue.")

It will probably take large numbers of us speaking up, though, to convince the airlines to provide all airplanes with a richer blend. And even so, it may still take legislation.

Everyone who flies is adversely affected by the airlines' cutting back on the fresh air. Every single function in the body is dependent upon our getting enough oxygen. Air travel can even be deadly for passengers with heart disease or pulmonary weakness,[11] and also for infants[12] whose tiny lungs make them most vulnerable when the air is recycled and there is not enough fresh oxygen. Passengers with impaired lung functioning and also multiple chemical sensitivities tell me they cannot survive in the commercial jet cabin without having their own private oxygen bottles.

Scientists have now proven that one symptom of oxygen deprivation is impaired vision.[13] The airlines, in their wisdom, of course want the pilots to see. Some airlines even instruct their pilots to sip pure oxygen prior to landing. Obviously, the airlines are aware of the detrimental effects of oxygen deprivation, but at this point, they won't even admit that oxygen-rich cockpits are for the pilots.

Airline management maintains that oxygen-rich cockpits are only for the computers.

On board, I clearly experience more body aches and mental angst when the air is recycled. I felt this over twenty years ago, before the facts were laid out. My sensitivity revealed to me that I could no longer take deep breaths, that my skin burned, that my back ached, and that my memory dissipated as a result of oxygen deprivation.

When I spoke up, most pilots told me I was imagining things. The more I spoke, the more flak I got. Some of my peers supported me, but many were confused by my actions, and they didn't want to make trouble. The flight attendants' union never backed me. They still have done nothing to help flight attendants and passengers get better air quality.

As a flight attendant, I used to go up to the cockpit to verify my perceptions with the control switches. Many pilots told me they thought I was meddling, so I developed strategies to find out what I wanted to know without annoying them: a fresh pitcher of water or leftovers from a first-class hors d'oeuvres cart offered to them while I checked out the air-quality control switches.

Sometimes, with pain in my lungs and frustration building in my psyche, I was tempted to flip the switches myself. Of course, I didn't do that. In-

Why airplane air is recycled

- Outside a jet, the air is unbreathable, whether the plane flies at 25,000 feet (for example, a commuter flight) or 60,000 feet (on the Concorde).

- The airplane's air packs pressurize outside, thin air until its density is approximately 8,000 feet (compact enough to breathe comfortably, according to the FAA, which does not permit commercial planes to fly with an interior cabin altitude over 8,000 feet).

- To save money, the airlines mix this pressurized, thin, fresh air with recycled (already-breathed) cabin air. With more recycled air, less fuel is needed to operate the air packs, so the operating cost of the flight is lower.

stead, I resorted to arguments with pilots. Most of them became defensive of their right to decide how much oxygen the passengers and I required. My position was that, while sitting in oxygen-rich cockpits, they were not qualified to judge if it was okay to cut back the air in the cabin.

An argument could be put forth that airplane air should not be decided by pilots, or CEO's, for that matter, who never fly in economy. Radicals argue that spoiled air on jets is simply a result of CEO "spoils" (salaries and golden parachutes). Forbes ranks airline CEO's among the top worldwide.[14] American's Crandall cleared $18.5 million over a five-year stretch. USAir's Wolf only got $672 thousand in 1996, but he already has a golden parachute from United to supplement his income. United's Greenwald took home $3.5 million.

The airlines publicly state there is no correlation between the quality of air in aircraft cabins and health problems.[15] Privately, the airlines say that there's always a compromise and certain things we have to endure because large numbers of people are being transported at rock bottom rates. *Does this justify cutting passengers' air to save $80 an hour in fuel costs?*

Until the flying public demands and supports only airline companies that provide 100% fresh air to everyone on board, the flying public is prey to these unsafe airline practices.

Legislation

Sitting in the U.S. Congress is proposed legislation offering airline passengers twice as much

fresh air as we are now getting. If passed, this legislation would bring passengers' air up to the standards of U.S. federal prisons.

But why should air standards for passengers be as low as those for convicts?

Passengers should not be treated like convicts. Legislators should insure that airline passengers get the same air quality standard that pilots get—which is ten times more air than passengers are now getting.[16]

Even minimal prison standards have not passed into law for passengers. But any law should include an enforcement provision, rather than just a toll free number to report travel-related illnesses, as the present proposed law does.

Perhaps the flying public could collaborate amongst themselves to monitor fresh airflow. Hand-held oxygen meters cost about $2000 each. How about fifty frequent flyers stepping forward to do the testing?

Air Quality: Symptoms you may experience

Blurred vision, bloating, body aches, breathing difficulties, clammy skin, coughing, depression, digestive upsets, ear problems, eye problems, fatigue, flu, giddiness, headache, nausea, numbness in extremities, poor concentration, rage, respiratory infection, shallow breathing, spacey, weakened immunity.

Air Quality: Strategies for self-defense

➤ Ask a flight attendant to convey to the pilot that you'd like the ventilation to be turned up to maximum capacity, that you'd like "full utilization of air." Alternately, and perhaps even more affective, write a note to the pilot and ask a flight attendant to deliver it. In the note, write your name and seat number and tell the pilot that you think the air is stuffy, that it is difficult to breathe, and whatever other symptoms you are experiencing.

➤ Reduce your chances of catching infections on jets by breathing through a wet hankie—your own hankie saturated with your own drinking water. This provides humidity for the delicate mucous membranes and cuts down on the transmission of diseases.

➤Optional: Wear a respirator with carbon filters. Available through building supply stores, these are worn by people working with toxic sprays and other situations where the air quality is compromised.

➤ It's always important to tell a flight attendant if you experience difficulty breathing. The plane could have a slow decompression.

➤ Tell a flight attendant if you have headache and joint pain. These could be early signals of the bends (if flying less than twenty-four hours after diving).

➤Remember: flight attendants breathe the same lousy air you do, and it's harder to think clearly when your brain doesn't get enough oxygen. Help flight attendants by offering exact change for in-flight headsets, drinks, and duty-free purchases.

➤ If you feel that your breaths are shallow and painful, and if you feel that the cabin air is stuffy, ask a flight attendant for an oxygen bottle. There is no charge for the bottle in these emergency situations.

➤Breath feeds the brain. Shallow breaths seem to coincide with racing thoughts. Deep breaths create a relaxed, peaceful, creative mind. The stresses of air travel are easier when we take deep breaths. Fill the abdomen with air and then let the air rise to the lungs. Then feel your abdomen press in when exhaling.

➤ If your seat has an air vent that is stuck in the open position, you can cover it with an emergency instruction folder taped across the corners to divert airflow. Ask a flight attendant to please bring you some tape; there's invariably some in the cockpit. If a vent is stuck in either the open or closed position, report this to a flight attendant. Malfunctions will be noted in the Aircraft Maintenance Log, so they will be fixed for the next passenger. (Sadly, though, with the cost-cutting airline policies, many maintenance items get deferred.)

➤ Sometimes you'll find the front of the cabin has more air. For the most part, though, the best air on board is where there are the least number of people. This is why the air is better in first class.

➤ Leave the plane during transit stops to get some fresh air and exercise.

➤ Some entrepreneur might consider oxygen booths in airports. A few good gulps helps with hypoxia associated with air travel. In Japan, oxygen vending machines are sometimes available to aid city dwellers seeking to alleviate metropolitan hypoxia.

➤ Write the airlines. Tell them that expensive ad campaigns touting award-winning cuisine don't make up for poor air quality, that you'd rather have the air than the bubbly. Or, suggest that they recycle the menus instead of the air. Send copies of your letter to your congressperson, to your newspaper, to yours truly, and to wherever else you think it might do some good.

➤ Spend some time every day breathing in fresh air: city parks, botanical gardens, by the shore. We rid ourselves of toxins with every exhalation. For more information about detoxification, I recommend you read my book, *NONI–Aspirin of the Ancients*.

Radiation—frequent flyers beware

➤ *Lobby against transporting radioactive materials as cargo on commercial jets.*

What is the first thing you think of when you hear the word "radiation"? Microwave oven? Hiroshima? But what about frequent flying?

Yes. We are frying in airplanes. Solar radiation passes right through the aluminum skin of jets and exposes passengers to dangerous doses of radiation. The problem is so alarming that Dr. Robert Barish, Chief of Radiotherapy at New York's Cancer Institute, warns, "Frequent flyers should be classified as occupationally-exposed radiation workers."[1]

When humans are exposed to radiation, they can be harmed at an atomic level. What this means to airline passengers is described in a 1991 FAA advisory[2] for people who fly frequently:

—Increased risk of cancer.
—Increased risk of birth defects in children resulting from parents' exposure to radiation before they conceived children.

—Increased risks of harm to children in the womb (mental retardation, developmental abnormalities, childhood cancers).

Some doctors advise pregnant flyers that it is especially dangerous to fly during the first eight weeks of pregnancy when the nervous system of the fetus is forming. Others say it is dangerous at any time during the pregnancy.

Where does radiation come from?

Radiation comes to us from many sources—from exploding stars, from nuclear power production and accidents, from bomb-testing fallout, X-rays, radar, smoke detectors, and radiopharmaceuticals.[3] We are also exposed to radiation throughout our computerized and cellular-phone world. Many of our helpful technologies produce radiation.

There are other surprising sources of toxic radiation, such as the glossy coating in magazines and an orange pottery glaze which actually contains more radioactive uranium than smoke detectors.[4]

The disturbing news is: radiation *is* cumulative. This is worth repeating. **The effects of harmful radioactive rays are cumulative.**

Our bodily accumulative exposure levels are

higher today than ever before—even before we step on airplanes. With this in mind, the Panel on Passenger Screening at the U.S. National Research Council recommends that "airlines offer alternative procedures for those who may not want to be irradiated [at airport security points]."[5]

Cancer & airline crew

Since 1990, airline crew members in the United States have been referred to by the industry as "occupationally-exposed radiation workers."

The airlines benefit from this classification because it allows pilots and flight attendants to have 50 times more radiation than if they were considered members of the general public. In other words, crew may now be exposed to 50 times more harmful radiation than is "allowed" for people who are not classified as occupationally-exposed radiation workers.

With this occupational classification, however, the airlines have been advised to fulfill two responsibilities to crew members:

1) Provide information about the health risks of radiation.

2) Regularly test everyone who is exposed—just as radiation workers in nuclear power plants are tested.

Surprisingly, exposures for crew members are greater than those incurred by nuclear power plant workers.[6] Unfortunately, testing and information have not been provided for crew by the airlines. The hazards of occupational radiation are not mentioned in training—not by the airlines, not by the FAA, and not by the unions.

Airline crews are the only group of radiation workers in the world who are exposed as part of their work to measurable doses of ionizing radiation and are neither educated nor tested.

Every other occupationally-exposed group gets education and testing—medical people who take X-rays, lab techs who scrub glassware, workers who clean pipes in oil fields, radiopharmaceutical people, smoke detector manufacturers, thousands of researchers in biology labs testing animals and performing DNA sequencing (like for OJ's trial). All these people are required to have radiation training and to be monitored by their employers. Yet, the highest exposed group—airline crew—is not treated in the same way.

There have been only a couple of independent studies on radiation among airline crew. One study of commercial pilots found that pilots have a higher incidence of rectum and brain cancer.[7] In another study, flight attendants were found to have twice the normal incidence of breast cancer.[8]

Breast cancer is more easily caused by radiation than any other kind of cancer.[9] It was also the most widespread cancer among Hiroshima survivors—*and* at exactly the same ratio to the general population as in the flight attendant study, 2:1. In Hiroshima, the atomic bomb left a giant dose of radiation in its wake causing death, cancer, and fetal anomalies. Today, air travelers are exposed over time to these same giant doses of radiation in long-term exposures.

One hundred years ago, when scientists first discovered x-rays, they noticed that radiation could burn up human tissues. They also noted a delay between the exposure and the burned skin.

It is known that radiation causes genetic defects[10] and breast cancer[11]—though the delay between the exposures and genetic defects and cancer is much more prolonged than the burned skin.

In the flight attendant breast cancer study, all the flight attendants with breast cancer had over fifteen years' seniority. Most senior flight attendants know a colleague who's died of breast cancer. One of my flying partners with eighteen years' seniority died of breast cancer.

Today, scientists say there is no safe dose of radiation.[12] Some people say the airlines hide behind the delayed-effects paradigm. It is difficult to pinpoint exposures and legal culpability of injury.

Check your mileage awards

If you average twenty hours per week in a jet, you are considered "significantly exposed." If you fly 75,000 miles (121,000 km) a year (a monthly trip from New York to London or two trips each month from Chicago to San Francisco), your employer is legally responsible to educate you about the risks. And you are entitled to medical monitoring due to increased risk of cancer, birth defects, and death—in the same way it is done in the nuclear power industry.

If classified as a "radiation sensitive worker," a frequent flyer would be permitted 50 times more radiation, just like crew. This classification implies that you accept the risk.

Recently, a passenger got burned by hot coffee and sued. Someday a passenger will sue for excessive and irresponsible radiation exposures. Today, however, you can scream until you glow in the dark. With the current attitude of the aviation industry, it will take more than one screamer to light *this* darkness.

Solar storms can equal 100 chest x-rays

Health hazard fact: Commercial flights are not terminated during solar storms.

During solar storms, harmful radiation rains on the residents of earth—and dangerously so on airline passengers traveling above the earth. Also, during solar storms, levels of radiation exceed the maximum permissible dose to prevent birth defects among pregnant flyers.[13]

On a typical commercial flight—when there are no solar storms—passengers between New York and London receive about a chest X-ray's[14] dose of harmful radiation. During solar storms, passengers can be bombarded with an equivalent of "one hundred chest X-rays," according to Dr. Barish, the New York Cancer Institute radiologist expert.

Not only that, but chest X-rays are limited to the area from navel to neck, so the organs at risk are only the breasts, lungs, and bone marrow. But in-flight radiation effects everything from the tip of the toes up—including the eyes and the thyroid, which is particularly sensitive to radiation.

The frequency of solar storms is in tandem with the eleven-year sunspot cycle. Scientists have recorded that every eleven years, there are excessive explosions on the sun. In 1989, during a peak, there were twenty-two solar storms. Another peak is predicted around the turn of the century—making this radiation information especially critical for frequent flyers, pregnant flyers, and crew.

It's a hard rain

The jet streams hold increased radiation. While the reasons remain unclear, passengers are exposed to twice the radiation in jet streams than above and below them.[15] Commercial jets fly inside the jet streams to save on fuel costs.

I would like to see the airlines notify passengers during solar storms, in case people want to cancel their flights.

Once passengers understand that radiation is to them as kryptonite is to Superman, they may want to ask their doctors to provide a note in case of a no-show, so they don't get a penalty on their tickets. We should be able to decide for ourselves if we want to fly during periods of quantum radiation.

Creative, practical solutions to reduce the effects of in-flight radiation are desperately needed for crew and frequent flyer protection. At present, I have no knowledge of any research being done in this area.

Lower radiation flights

Plan your flights with radiation exposures in mind. Radiation doubles every 6,500 feet (2,000 meters),[16] so flights at lower altitudes have less radiation. For example, the Los Angeles-London nonstop has more radiation than the flight which transits New York.[17]

The jets that fly highest have more radiation, and you will find them on the long-range non-stops: Boeings' 747SP, 747-400 and 767-300ER, Airbus A340-200, MD11, and, of course, the Concorde. Radiation on the Concorde is greater than in any other aircraft because of its altitude. The Concorde is only flown by British Airways and Air France, and the latter has announced that it is planning to phase out its Concordes because of high maintenance costs.[18]

Flights at lower latitudes also have less radiation than flights over the Poles. Flights near or around the equator have the least radiation.

Since a large part of the harmful radiation in jets originates from the sun, some passengers ask if there is less exposure on night flights. Scientists say that the harmful radiation for passengers is the same on night flights as on day flights because our planet is awash in a cosmic wave of radiation from the sun— as if the Earth were a beach ball in the ocean.

Toxic cargo

Another source of on-board toxic radiation is found in commercial jet cargo holds. "In the United States during 1975, radioactive material was transported on about one of every thirty passenger flights."[19] Recent statistics are not available, but radioactive material still flies at jet cargo.

Passengers concerned about on-board radiation exposure might consider lobbying against this practice.

Sea vegetables

Now that my heavy flying days are behind me, I still keep in mind the sum total of radiation I accumulated during that period. For this reason, I still avoid X-rays when I can, I swim in the ocean as often as possible to pull the radiation out through the pores, and I favor seaweed in my diet.

Sea vegetables are known natural antidote to radiation. A lot of this information came originally from Japan where seaweed is said to have saved lives in Hiroshima.

Radiation: Symptoms you may experience

Birth defects, cancer, headache, nausea, subclinical pathologies, weakened immunity.

Radiation: Strategies for self-defense

➤When planning your flight routing, choose flights at lower latitudes and lower altitudes.

➤All your personal effects in your carry-ons are exposed to radiation at airport security checkpoints. You can hand them personally to the security staff and ask for a visual inspection instead—for food, supplements, water, and also your computer. Even if the security agent tells you that "The amount of radiation will have no effect...," you can insist on a visual inspection instead of radiation—politely, of course.

➤Drink a lot of water to flush, lubricate, and vitalize the body's own electrical charge.

➤Passengers may want to cancel their flights during solar storms. Cancel flights without a penalty with a note from your doctor. Information about solar storms can be accessed at the Space Environment Services Center (303/497-3235) on a daily updated one-minute recording. If there is a solar storm, the recorded message will say, "A solar particle event has occurred." The event can last from a couple of days up to a couple of weeks.

➤Take baking soda/sea salt baths or swim in the ocean to draw out toxins through the pores.

➤Lobby your government:

- Against transporting radioactive materials as cargo on commercial jets.

- To mandate that during solar storms commercial aircraft must reduce their altitude or terminate their flights.

- To mandate that businesses educate their employees who fly about radiation and its risks, as well as test those employees for accumulated radiation.

Ozone

➤ *Passengers with respiratory ailments and pulmonary diseases may prefer to avoid long-range, high-altitude flights.*

We can deal with some of the hazardous conditions on jets as soon as we learn about them, like putting a hankie over your nose to stop the spread of germs. Unfortunately, there are other hazards which will require government policy changes and aircraft design corrections to protect passengers. Ozone poisoning is one of these.

Toxic ozone seeps into jetliners at high altitudes, triggering coughing, headaches, burning eyes, and troubled breathing.[1]

Ominous ozone

At a Hearing in the U.S. Congress on ozone pollution, passengers and crew testified that sometimes their chest pains were so acute a heart attack was suspected.[2]

More often, though, ozone gas just increases

our susceptibility to respiratory infections and weakens passengers by damaging the lungs.[3]

According to the U.S. Environmental Protection Agency, repeated ozone exposures for crew and frequent flyers can lead to permanent lung scarring and loss of lung functioning.[4]

Ozone damage is directly related to the amount of activity one has while breathing poisonous ozone gas. Obviously, this is why flight attendants were the first to start screaming (with hoarse voices) about shortness of breath, chest pain, and coughing. Due to the aerobic nature of taking care of passengers in the thin air, flight attendants inhale about four times as much ozone as the passengers or the pilots.[5]

Commercial jets fly as high as possible because the thinner the air outside, the less fuel it takes to fly. With the introduction of the long-haul high-altitude flight, ozone complaints increased.[6] Scientists found that ozone is present at higher altitudes primarily in the spring in the Northern Hemisphere and in the fall in the Southern Hemisphere. It is always dense close to the Poles.

Although aircraft are now theoretically equipped with ozone-destroying catalytic filters, a 1994 Harvard study found that up to 20% of flights had noxious ozone levels.[7]

The Aviation Clear Air Act of 1996 proposed that the FAA issue stronger regulations relating to "monitoring of ozone levels in the cabin." The Act was never passed. Meanwhile, frequent flyers and flight attendants are the biological equivalent of an in-place monitoring system. It appears that those who enact laws to protect people's health and well-being are as lackadaisical about in-flight ozone as they are about damaging the ozone layer itself—humans are still damaging the ozone layer, and the ozone is still damaging humans who fly!

Although most ozone gas remains in the ozone layer twenty to thirty miles above the earth, feather-like wisps of ozone extend down to jet altitudes—a direct result of the damage to the ozone layer.

What is ironic is that the very same ozone layer, when we are below it, rather than in it, protects us from the harmful effects of ultraviolet radiation. It is our essential sunblock. Would that we could block the damage to the ozone layer and all live happily ever after.

The Concorde soars the highest of all commercial jets, around 60,000 feet. There, the threat of ozone and radiation contamination is also the highest of any commercial passenger airplane.

Concordephiles claim that dangers are offset by the supersonic's reduced flight time.

Concordephobes retort that the supersonic's high-altitude emissions of sulfuric acid now cause more damage to the ozone layer than all the fluorocarbons deployed on Earth. As a matter of fact, it is common knowledge that supersonic and subsonic aircraft are significantly, directly responsible for destroying the ozone layer.[8]

Scientists say that high-altitude ozone and radiation react together[9] creating a venomous poison. As with many toxins, it is only realistic to look at their synergistic and cumulative effects.

The entire flying experience needs to be rethought in terms of healthy flying. Healthy flying can no longer be separated out from safe flying. People are getting ill after being on airplanes. Airline safety must always include healthy flying.

Ozone: Symptoms you may experience

Burning eyes, chest pain, coughing, difficulty breathing, dizziness, eye problems, faintness, fatigue, headache, nosebleeds, shortness of breath, spitting up blood, sore throat, spacey, susceptibility to illness, weakened immunity.

Ozone: Strategies for self-defense

➤ Passengers with respiratory and pulmonary ailments may do well to avoid long-range, high-altitude flights.

➤ Lobby your government:

- Ozone levels should be monitored on all flights. When there is excessive ozone, flights need to be automatically re-routed with changes in altitude and latitude.

- "Acceptable" standards for in-flight ozone should be more stringent.

- Pilots should be required to employ "full utilization of air" at all times—especially when ozone is detected on board.

- Flight attendants and passengers should monitor and report the cabin air comfort level according to their own sense of well-being.

Pesticide Showers

> ➤ *If you are pregnant, asthmatic, or allergic to pesticide, you may be able to get off the plane before they spray the cabin with insecticide.*

Today, many international passengers will be treated to a shower of pesticide before they are permitted to put even one toe on solid ground. This macabre, mandatory landing ritual is, in fact, currently performed in dozens of nations. (See the complete list on the next page.)

It is clearly illegal for someone to wrestle me to the ground, pry open my lips, and pour solvent down my throat. Yet I may be required to sit quietly with my seatbelt fastened while a flight attendant sprays poison a few inches above my head, so the mist of poison rains down on my skin, hair, and clothes.

Killer mist

About thirty minutes before arrival, you'll hear a quick announcement about the "disinsection" (literally: to get rid of insects).

Countries: pesticides & passengers

- **Before or After Landing:** Grenada, India, Kiribati, Madagascar, Trinidad and Tobago require that pesticide is sprayed on passengers every flight. Before landing: spraying is done by flight attendants, the plane's air conditioning is *on*. After landing: spraying is done by local authorities, air conditioning is *off*, and sometimes passengers can also get off. Sprayers walk up the aisle emptying two cans of pesticide, aiming between the overhead bins and the top of passengers' heads.

- **After takeoff:** Switzerland and the U.K. require that pesticide is sprayed on passengers on certain sectors, including flights from Egypt, Nigeria, and the Seychelles. Spraying is done after takeoff by attendants.

- **Residual spraying:** Australia, Barbados, Fiji, Jamaica and New Zealand require pesticide sprayed in empty airplanes every eight weeks. The pesticide, permithrin, is banned in the U.S. because it is a suspected carcinogen that damages the liver and lungs. Its residual presence saturates all cabin furnishings.

During the last few years that I was flying, I fell ill on every flight after pesticide was sprayed. Within hours of spraying, my eyes dripped yellow pus. I also suffered a loss of coordination, making me fall down and drop things. I continued in this way for a year, using my days off to recover with the aid of antibiotics and bed rest.

My flying days ended when my body no longer responded to the medication. I suffered backaches, headaches, fevers, fatigue, and chronic eye, ear, and staph infections.

I was diagnosed with MCS (multiple chemical sensitivity), a breakdown of the body's ability to detoxify. This condition is triggered by exposure to a poison delivered either in one crippling dose or in repeated small doses. Common chemicals found in window cleaner, hair spray, deodorant, perfume, paint, plastic, dry-cleaning, detergent, car exhaust, and news print can trigger severe allergic reactions. My doctor clearly attributes my "acute sensitivity" to the pesticides in my former workplace (jet cabins).

When is the cabin sprayed?

It is rumored that flight attendants, unbeknownst to passengers, spray pesticide into the air-conditioning ducts. I have never seen this. I do know that some attendants, out of compassion for the passengers, discharge the cans behind closed lav doors (the only space on board where the out-flowing air is dumped overboard instead of recycled back in.) The cans must be emptied (six for every 747). They are collected after landing as proof.

Some countries do the spraying themselves after landing. This is more hazardous for us because the air-conditioning is off. However, it is possible for a passenger to get off before the spraying begins. Present a note from your doctor saying that you are asthmatic, pregnant, or allergic to pesticide. No other circumstances seem to deliver exemptions.

The newest trend among airlines is to spray planes every eight weeks with a pesticide called permithrin. Deployed in an empty aircraft, this guarantees uncomplaining and uninformed passengers. When the spraying is completed, the air-conditioning is supposed to be operated for a minimum of one hour before passengers board. *What do you think?* If a pesticide's off-gassing is strong enough to kill insects for eight weeks, surely it is strong enough to be toxic to the passengers who breathe the residual fumes during those eight weeks—especially the first couple of days after each application.

There is a second type of residual spraying which occurs in the U.S. at the last airport before a plane leaves for the Bahamas, Granada, Barbados, Bermuda, Jamaica, Trinidad, Panama, Argentina, Uruguay. Prior to every flight, every day, this toxic residue builds up on passengers' seats, especially on airplanes that regularly fly these routes. The insecticide is d-Phenothrin—actually the product Black Knight Roach Killer wearing a different label. The label offers this disheartening advice to air travelers: "Dangerous to humans. Avoid breathing vapors. If inhaled, remove victim to fresh air."

Cargo compartments are also routinely bombed. Our checked luggage gets contaminated, which permits the poison to penetrate to our effects. Hard cases absorb less.

Officially, the governments that require insecticidation claim that the pesticiding of passengers from foreign lands will prevent the spread of plant and animal diseases to their lands.[1]

An airport official in New Zealand explained to me that their pesticide is not harmful to humans, nor is it even designed to kill pests, only stun them!

What about those stunned bugs that fall inert into pant cuffs only to wake up refreshed in a closet at the Auckland Sheraton? The spray is clearly not an effective bug deterrent. However, having been sprayed a hundred times, I am here to testify and, in fact, I have testified that it definitely stuns humans.

Pesticide: Symptoms you may experience

Anxiety, bloated organs, body aches, burning eyes, burning skin, chest pain, confusion, depression, dizziness, fetal birth defects, headache, impaired coordination, irritability, memory loss, modified reaction to drugs, nausea, nervous tension, shaking uncontrollably, shortened attention span, shortness of breath, sore throat, thirst, weakened immunity.

Pesticide: Strategies for self-defense

➤Pack your clothes inside plastic bags. After landing, trash the plastic and clean your luggage before carrying it indoors, especially before placing on your bed to unpack.

➤Travel in a long-sleeve shirt and trousers so the toxicity in the seat cushions won't rub into your skin.

➤Get a note from your doctor if you're pregnant, asthmatic, or allergic to pesticide. Use it to disembark before the spraying beings.

➤If you can't disembark before the spraying, as soon as possible after takeoff, ask the purser if there is going to be pesticide sprayed, and when. Travel with a plastic fold-up raincoat that you can get under during pesticiding and then dispose of on the airplane, or cover yourself with an airline blanket. This will reduce somewhat the amount of pesticide that you will absorb through your skin into your body, as well as the amount you will retain in your clothes and hair where off-gassing will continue to release toxins into your lungs.

➤If pesticide exposure is a grave issue for you, carry a respirator. Use of airline oxygen bottles is not viable because the masks have holes that admit cabin air.

➤Airplanes treated with residual spray can show up on any route. The certificate of residual spray with its date of application can be found on board in first class, inside the forward left-hand coat closet.

➤Join the worldwide wave protesting pesticide spray. Wield economic power as a repellent against nations that use volatile bug bombs. Write to the embassies and tourism bureaus and protest.

➤Write to Congress. Insist that there be notification so that people can make informed choices. Information about spraying pesticides on passengers and in aircraft cabins should be printed in airline schedules and in all advertisements and also related verbally upon ticket inquiry and in writing upon ticket sale.

Toxic Chemicals

➤ *Reduce your everyday exposures to toxins so that you are stronger when you have to enter a toxic environment, such as the jet cabin.*

It is common knowledge today that many commercial practices pollute our world. Yet we may not be aware that the toxic chemicals which are used to make up quite a number of everyday products can cause illness and even death if there is little or no fresh air around us when we use these products.

People are exposed to potentially damaging toxic chemicals, for example, with drain cleaners, spot removers, art and craft supplies, cleaning compounds, nail polishes, paint and paint thinners, antifreeze, adhesives, fabric softeners, fabric finishes, and printers' ink. (Less-polluting, soy-based ink is used to print this book.)

On jets, in the enclosed cabins with reduced fresh air, the fabric finish on seats and carpets and the plastics used in bulkheads, tray tables, and armrests are all sources of toxicity. **Plastics, when new, actually out-gas poisonous fumes.** "If one could see the molecular activity on the surface of an active material, such as some plastics and paints, it would appear to be slowly boiling, releasing a cloud of gas into the surrounding air."[1]

Adhesives and the stain resistant solution used in carpeting are also toxic in airplanes. Composite materials used to in manufacturing aircraft and chemicals used to make aircraft interiors flame resistant are also making people ill. As a matter of fact, there is a pending class action lawsuit brought by employees at Boeing. The workers, who claim they were poisoned, experienced symptoms of burning eyes, skin sores, chest pain, disorientation, and brain damage.[2]

Love Canal and the jet stream

Class action suits have now been initiated by flight attendants for toxic exposures, too. Flight attendants at Alaska Airlines claim fumes from hydraulic fluid are sucked into the cabin air. More than 600 of the airline's 1,575 flight attendants have reported health problems, including headaches, nausea, and chemical sensitivities.[3] Similarly, in Australia, over sixty flight attendants say they suffer from nausea, vomiting, irritated eyes, and other problems because of oil fumes in the cabin.[4] Despite this, sick planes continue to fly, the public is not informed, the airlines maintain that the fumes are not toxic.

Frequent flyers are also at risk, but, because symptoms of chemical poisoning can be delayed, many passengers get ill after landing without understanding that their flu-like symptoms are actually indications of toxic chemical poisoning.

From time to time, accounts of toxic vapors in jets reach the news media. For example, a hydraulic fluid leak on a Continental flight caused passengers to be evacuated.[5] Similarly, a USAirways flight made an emergency landing and seven people were taken to the hospital with chest pain caused by fumes.[6]

Routine toxic exposures include the smell of aviation gasoline, especially on runways prior to take-off when idling engines emit higher percentages of carbon monoxide, oxides of nitrogen, hydrocarbons, aldehydes, and polynuclear aromatic compounds.[7] Some passengers write to me that they get sick on flights after de-icing chemicals are applied.

Another source of toxic fumes is the cargo hold. Hazardous materials are transported on commercial jets. Noxious fumes can enter the passengers' air supply if these materials topple or leak.[8]

One such leak occurred in 1997 on an American Airlines flight from Miami to Ecuador—passengers became sick with burning eyes and lungs and the aircraft had to be evacuated.[9]

The FAA promised to improve oversight of hazardous material after the 1996 ValuJet crash, but there were over 1,600 reported violations of hazardous material shipments in 1998.[10] One leak on a British Airways flight sent twenty-five people to the hospital.[11] Hazardous materials, which are regularly shipped on commercial jets, include paints, flammable liquids, adhesives, pesticides, and fireworks. Vials of viruses and germs also crisscross the world as cargo on commercial jets.[12]

Many people have now become chemically sensitized. This is a condition caused by damage to the body from toxic chemicals. For an easy-to-understand explanation of this condition, turn to "How Toxins Affect Us," written by James Miller, M.D., on page 387.

Thousands of doctors today support my 1992 allegation in JET SMART that the toxicity in commercial jet cabins can be disabling to anyone who spends a significant amount of time in that environment.

Personal chemicals on the airplane

A little known but highly toxic source of poisoning in jet cabins is the personal chemicals worn by passengers and crew. These chemicals drift into the cocktail of poisonous chemicals that passengers

134

What chemical sensitization feels like

- It's like driving along and suddenly your wheels spin because you're in "neutral" and the car won't shift back into "drive" even if you could remember how to operate the shift.

- It's how whales feel when they beach themselves and behave erratically, and how eagles feel when they can't do anything about the fact that their species is dying out because their egg shells are too thin.

- It's like being jetlagged, and you just got fired *and* also heard that your father died.

have to breathe on board. Yes. Poisonous. Designer fragrances actually contain nerve poisons that aren't regulated,[13] and up to 30% of Americans (75 million people) report that they may be allergic to perfumes and dry-cleaned clothes.[14]

Until the airlines find ways to provide passengers with adequate fresh air, thoughtful air travelers should avoid perfume, scented personal products such as hair spray and lotion, dry-cleaned clothes, and clothes dried with scented fabric softener. Please.

Toxic Chemical: Symptoms you may experience

Bloated organs, body aches, burning eyes, chest pain, coughing, dizziness, fatigue, headache, impaired co-ordination, memory loss, nausea, nervous tension, sore throat, spaciness, weakened immunity.

Toxic Chemicals: Strategies for self-defense

➤Regularly cleanse—detoxify—yourself of toxic buildup in your tissues and organs. You may want to read my book on detoxification, NONI: *Aspirin of the Ancients.*

➤In your daily life, practice deep breathing. By exercising your body's ability to function on a held breath, you can buy yourself valuable seconds if there is a release of toxic chemicals in your environment. You may also want to read my book, *Office Yoga: A quickie guide to staying balanced and fit in the work environment.*

➤Reduce everyday toxic exposures so that your system is less compromised before flying. Take a look at your exposures to printer's ink, adhesives, cleaning compounds, petrochemicals, and personal care products—perfumes, nail polish, antiperspirants, hair conditioners, fabric softeners, and pesticides.

EMF–electromagnetic fields

➤ *To help ameliorate the effects of EMF, eat chlorophyll-rich greens.*

A recent issue of global controversy centers on the invisible pollution known as EMF. Electromagnetic fields (like the charismatic actor of old, W.C. Fields) have their own unique electric charge and magnetic attraction. In the latter, the attraction is believed to be fatal. Reports of cancer and miscarriages[1] due to the supression of the immune system[2] are on file.

When I became chemically sensitive, I found I had also acquired a heightened feel for EM fields. This serious health hazard causes headache, fever, light-headedness, and short-term cognitive memory loss.

I first became aware of this energy when I lived within a few miles of a military base, which used a radar surveillance system. Whenever I drove within its range, I promptly became ill. Acute sensitivity like mine is unusual, but it "exists as a definite clinical entity," explains cardiovascular surgeon and environmental expert, William Rea, MD.[3]

Electric-shock therapy

It is well known that EM pulses can be used to affect behavior. Electro-shock therapy is one application. Another application, used in the sixties, was concocted by the Soviets, who regularly "stimulated" the U.S. Moscow Embassy and succeeded in modifying the behavior of those who worked there.[4]

EMF in aviation

EMF activity is most dense in the vicinity of international airports with microwave landing systems and less dense in airports where they only have microwave fast-food ovens!

On jets, EM pollution is caused by radar— ground and airborne—cockpit computers, jet engines, and the electrical wiring throughout an aircraft. The newer 777's offer individual TV monitors in the seat backs. These LCD flat panel displays create an extremely intense local EMF only three inches behind the spine—a critical part of the nervous system—of the person seated in front of them.

Electrical wiring may be even more dangerous. Swiss Air decided to shut down its high-tech entertainment systems after Flight 111 plunged into the Atlantic off Canada's east coast killing over two hundred (9-98). The entertainment system allows first-class and business-class passengers to watch movies, play electronic games and engage in interactive shopping. A probe into the cause of the crash found heat-damaged wires.[5]

At this time, there is no information available on the sources and/or effects of EM pulsations in commercial airline cabins. But it is possible that the airlines' disregard for the effects of EM fields on commercial aircraft has resulted in behavioral problems among crew and passengers.

There has been substantial research, however, into the various sources of EM pollution closer to the ground, affording us a lot of reasons to feel frazzled in everyday life! EM pulses emanate whenever there is electricity—dimmer switches, TVs, computers, X-rays, radar, power lines, hair dryers, refrigerators, elevators—all the electric smog of our high-tech life.

"Some of the European governments have standards which restrict exposure to levels which are one thousand times less than ours."[6] The Office of Technology Assessment advises "prudent avoidance."[7]

Today, aviation engineers admit that menstrual cycles of flight attendants are probably affected by EM fields in jets. It's the iron content in our blood, they suspect, which is pulled toward the fields and then clumps, as iron filings do.

English muffin standard

Until such time as adequate standards and safeguards are established for EMF exposures in jets, it appears unfair for flight attendants and passengers to be governed by obsolete exposure guidelines such as the English muffin standard: "the implication that microwave radiation was harmless as long as you didn't turn brown or feel toasty."[8]

All flyers will be well served when research on the cabin environment gives evidence of sources, sites, and incidence of significant EMF exposures.

Strengthen your own field

What helps to keep me functional in the world's highly-charged environment is a diode, an unassuming, inch-and-a-half square tile that "enhances the aura surrounding the body," according to visionary Wayne Cook,[9] who spent thirty-two years researching things like biomagnetic force fields.

In 1989, *Sharper Image Catalog* featured a diode pad which they suggested airline passengers sit on to offset jetlag. They discontinued it the following year. It didn't sell well because the model they promoted was too bulky for travel. A smaller diode can more easily slip into pockets and underwear, and is

140

more convenient for air travel—although I sit on a diode pad at my computer. Diodes are not necessarily for jetlag, but rather for the EM pulses encountered at airports and on jets.

EMF: Symptoms you may experience

Burning skin, confusion, digestive problems, fatigue, fetal birth defects, flu-like symptoms, headache, impatience, nausea, nervous tension, shaking, susceptibility to illness, weakened immunity.

EMF: Strategies for self-defense

➤To help ameliorate the effects of both non-ionizing radiation (EMF) and ionizing (cosmic) radiation:

- Drink a lot of water to flush, lubricate, and vitalize the body's own electrical charge.
- Take baking soda/sea salt baths after landing to draw out toxins through the pores.
- Eat chlorophyll-rich greens, (spinach, seaweed, chard, kale, etc.).[10]

High Altitude

> ➤ *Health conditions which may be affected by on-board low air pressure include cardiovascular, pulmonary, and gastro-intestinal weaknesses.*

At high altitudes, air is "thin" with fewer oxygen molecules. This is significant to all passengers on commercial jets and especially people with pulmonary weakness, chemical sensitivities, and heart conditions. One study showed that 6-7% of people with ischemic (lack of blood) heart disease actually die after they travel by air.[1]

The director of the Aerospace Medical Association advises people who have just had a heart attack not to fly at all. "The person who has had a recent heart attack and who wants to hop on an airplane to recuperate in the Caribbean is asking for trouble."[2]

Flying high, feeling low

When we fly, all the tissues in our bodies swell up with nitrogen gas.[3] According to the experts, we expand about 35% at 8,000 feet.[4] Most jets that fly transcontinental and trans-oceanic maintain an "interior altitude" of 8,000 feet. The only aircraft that fly with a lower interior altitude are the commuter planes.

Airlines say they are not capable of creating an interior altitude equivalent to sea level. It's easy to understand why they don't want to—sea-level air weighs more, and weight costs money for the airlines. In addition, because outside air is too thin for passengers to breathe, it must be compressed on board, and that is another expense the airlines like to avoid—taking the thin air from outside and compressing it before pumping it into the cabin also costs the airlines money.

Why people swell up on airplanes

The low-pressure, high-altitude air on flights causes our bodies to swell up. This is why many people's ankles and feet swell. Have you ever kicked off your shoes at cruise altitude only to discover you couldn't get them back on after landing?

When I was a flight attendant, our uniform required us to have two pairs of shoes; we wore high heels for prancing through airports and low heels for pushing carts on board. I always wondered why the guys who loaded those 300-pound carts wore heavy, rubber-soled shoes, while we women, for the same labor, were required to wear heels with slippery leather soles. I also wondered why my in-flight shoes were always too tight—until I discovered that my in-flight shoes had to be half a size larger than those I wore on the ground because of the low air pressure in flight. Subsequent research revealed that it was the low air pressure which caused my feet—and every other part of my body—to swell after takeoff.

Deep-sea divers may be among the first on board to notice the changes of air pressure. Early signals of the bends—which can occur aloft if flying less than twenty-four hours after diving—are headache and joint pain. In this event, the pilot must be notified immediately because if a lower altitude is not taken, the passenger could die.

De-pressurized before landing

The airplane cabin is pressurized on takeoff and the interior altitude remains 8,000 feet throughout the flight. Then the plane is de-pressurized before landing, i.e. the air pressure is equalized to that of the arrival airport.

As an aircraft descends, the pilot raises the cabin altitude similar to the way deep-sea divers incrementally increase air pressure in their diving suits.

The airplane interior altitude on landing is set for slightly more than the elevation at the arrival airport in order to be able to open the aircraft's plug-type doors. If the altitude were always returned to sea level, and a plane landed in Mexico City or Denver (8,000 feet altitude), for example, when the forward entry door was opened, the heavier interior air would blast the agent to the other side of the airport.

High Altitude: Symptoms you may experience

Anxiety, breathing problems, circulatory problems, digestive disorders, disorientation, ear pain, fatigue, headache, hemorrhoids, hyperventilation, irregular heartbeat, joint pain, light-headedness, memory loss, nausea, nose bleed, poor concentration, shortness of breath, swollen feet, vertigo, visual disorientation.

High Altitude: Strategies for self-defense

➤Use massage to stimulate circulation. Massaging your feet and legs increases circulation. If I were to travel with a small child, I would massage his or her legs about once an hour and also encourage the child to move around.

➤Cayenne pepper and niacin are herbal home remedies for boosting circulation that I have found help-

146

ful, but frequent exercise on board is the most essential factor to increase circulation.

➤Air travelers with health conditions which may be affected by low air pressure such as cardiovascular, pulmonary, or gastrointestinal weaknesses, and also multiple chemical sensitivities, should consult a physician familiar with aviation medicine.

➤Possibly the doctor would recommend that you take "supplemental oxygen" when you fly. This must be ordered in advance and costs about $80 a bottle. You will also need a note from your doctor with a prescription for the oxygen "flow rate." The oxygen bottles have "high" and "low" flow rates. On the "low" setting, one bottle provides enough oxygen for a five-hour flight. The doctor's note will also need to certify that you are "fit to fly."

➤It's best to take your rings off before your fingers expand. Bring a zippered case specifically dedicated for precious items. After your body expands and contracts, and after you're jetlagged and un-jetlagged, at least you'll know where to find your jewelry.

➤Buy travel shoes which are half a size too big. Use cushion inserts for ground wear; then at cruise altitude, take out the inserts as your feet swell up. If you have shoelaces, loosen them in flight to avoid damaging the veins in your feet.

➤Avoid shallow breathing when you fly. Conscious breathing, exerting awareness and muscular strength to inhale/exhale fully and deeply, helps get more oxygen to the brain to maintain well-being. Conscious breathing is effective in flight, during transits, and especially after landing, right before sleep.

➤Here is an exercise to help you avoid hemorrhoids caused by low air pressure in commercial jets. Imagine you are pinching a penny between your buttocks. *Inhale.* Pull in your coin slot. Count to four. Release. *Exhale.* Do this anytime and often on your travel day, sitting or standing.

Dehydration

> ➤ *On your travel day, drink one large glass of water for every hour you are in transit, i.e., from home until you arrive at your hotel.*

On long-distance, high-altitude flights, humidity can drop to one percent,[1] much of that coming from your fellow passengers' lungs.

By comparison, in the Arabian desert where Lawrence of Arabia suffered from dehydration, there is a relative humidity of 11-21%.[2]

It is obvious that there is no way to avoid the fact that your body will become dehydrated when flying long distances on commercial jets. Symptoms can include light-headedness, dry skin and red eyes. So drink water. But not the plane's water, which is replenished wherever the aircraft lands and is not subject to any standard. Carry your own water.

Failing to drink the recommended 8 ounces of water per hour of flight and dehydrating yourself further with booze and coffee may cause the kidneys to reabsorb urine.

Every cell in the body is dependent on water. It is water that brings us nutrients from our food, and we are dependent on water to eliminate waste by-products. Water helps our brains think clearly by assisting the neurotransmitters to fire promptly.

In infants, water is about 75% of body mass. The proportion drops to about 40% as we get older. The thought that looking old might have something to do with not drinking enough water can really motivate some people (of course, I mean me) to drink more water.

Without adequate water intake, both health and inspiration quickly deteriorate. Perhaps water itself is the fountain of youth.

Fitness experts tell us that if you wait until you are thirsty, you're already dehydrated.[3] When you are an airline passenger, it is especially important not to wait until you feel thirsty.

There is no humidity introduced on board by the airlines. Humidity is there only incidentally from the departure airport as the aircraft doors seal in aspects of that environment prior to takeoff.

In other words, for a couple of hours after takeoff, flights leaving humid Honolulu, where the air is practically liquid, always have a higher relative humidity than flights leaving arid airports like Arizona and Arabia.

To pee or not to pee. Yes, pee.

Jet dehydration is essentially remedied by drinking eight to sixteen ounces of water for every hour of travel. The longer the flight, the more water we need. Carry your own bottled water. On board, there is rarely enough bottled water for all those who request it. Supplies have simply not kept pace with demand, or the airlines prefer to carry saleable supplies, like beer, hard liquor, and wine.

Occasionally, on longhauls, aircraft run completely dry—no water for coffee, or even for flushing. It's smart to be prepared: bring your own water when you fly. In addition, request a full bottle or can of water from your flight attendant during every bar and meal service. By drinking the bottled water supplies on board, you can save your own for transits, and for when beverages are not available, such as right before landing or during transit stops. You might tell them you'd like to open the bottle yourself. *The Wall Street Journal* reported that "United Airlines uses bottled water containers to serve tap water in business class on international routes."[4]

Carbonated or plain? Sometimes, carbonated water helps balance intestinal gas. Otherwise, purified or mineral water without gas best helps us to offset dehydration when we fly.

Skin tight

Dry skin is a side effect of flying. Even Miss America, Marjorie Vincent, when she was only twenty-one years old, got "those little lines around her eyes" after she'd been in the air for a few hours.[5]

Dehydration also shows up in the whites of the eyes—leaving those telltale streaks like crimson jet trails through the sky of the eye.

Don't be shy about protecting yourself

Once the departure city's humidity evaporates from the passenger cabins, the only moisture generated on board is from the breath and perspiration of the passengers and crew. In this sense, the more crowded the plane, the more humid the cabin remains—but, unfortunately, adding to the risk of contagious disease transmission. The latest information from the U.S. Centers for Disease Control (CDC) advises people with tuberculosis (15 million Americans) to avoid long flights on commercial airlines.

Some diseases enter the immune system through tiny cracks in the nasal passages when they become enlarged and raw in the dry cabin, so coat the inside of your nostrils with an edible oil to help prevent cracking. (Almond and olive oil are excellent for this.) Of course, wash your hands with soap and hot water before you touch the inside of your nose.

Another helpful way to block the transmission of contagious diseases is to cover your nose and mouth with a water-saturated, cotton handkerchief. Many doctors agree with me that this is over 90% effective in blocking the spread of germs. (I spoke at a medical convention where I surveyed about 100 doctors, and they all agreed that moistened hankies are more effective than dry ones for blocking the transmission of contagious diseases.)

A moistened hankie over your nose and mouth when you fly also provides humidity for your lungs. It's easy to wear a folded hankie by wrapping the ends around your ears. You might feel self-conscious. Are your seatmates snickering? So what! After flying, you will arrive healthy and many of them will have days of downtime with flu symptoms.

The speed with which moisture evaporates from this hankie will give you some idea of the degree of the aircraft's dryness. As an experiment, you can also try bringing a wet swimsuit in your carry-on—if it hasn't dried, and you have to leave for the airport, give this a try. Take your swimsuit out a few hours after takeoff and just tuck a corner in the seat-pocket in front of you. With near-zero humidity, drying is almost instantaneous.

"In normal conditions, we exhale approximately 20% of our water intake. Aboard long flights, this figure will rise to almost 50%."[6] In extreme cases, **if you get dehydrated, the brain sends an SOS to the kidneys, which then re-absorb water from your urine, setting in motion a radical state of affairs involving "at least 100 biochemical and hormonal rhythms in the body"[7] including, paradoxically, fluid retention.**

Today, the technology for humidifying jets is readily available; such equipment is optional at Boeing. But to sustain a comfortable humidity of 35%, for example, a 747 needs to weigh-in with 2200 pounds (1000 kg.) more water on takeoff.[8] When faced with the choice of humidified air or fifteen extra passengers, the airlines' priorities are consistent and clear.

Coffee, tea, or......?

So what's the healthiest drink on board? For passengers, ironically, airline beverage carts do not abound with a fine selection of the world's choice mineral waters or even bottles of purified water. In fact, the bar service on board offers a big selection of drinks that compound jetlag, such as carbonated soft drinks, canned juices, and, of course, alcohol.

Carbonated soft drinks can cause intestinal

154

gas, because all gases expand at high altitudes. Moreover, the sugar content can intensify low blood sugar levels, which are already a concern as our adrenal glands are racing into new time zones.

Orange juice could be a good occasional choice, but it's usually prepared on board, using one part concentrate to three parts tap water (which is suspect), and the concentrate is sweetened.

The airlines also offer coffee and black tea at every service. In addition to being made with tap water, coffee and black tea have diuretic properties, making the reality of in-flight dehydration even more intense. However, for those passengers who love a hot cup of coffee, here's how to get one. Walk back to any galley and ask a flight attendant to give you freshly made hot coffee in a paper crew cup. Cold coffee is a problem in jets because, at high altitudes, coffee boils at about 180 degrees Fahrenheit, instead of the normal 212 degrees. Also, the porcelain and plastic cups used to serve it are usually refrigerated on meal service tray.

Smart-class passengers walk back to the galley about once an hour to combat dehydration and muscle fatigue. Ask any attendant there to fix you a drink. If your preference is non-alcoholic (herbal tea bags or miso soup packets that you carry on board, for example), ask permission to make it yourself.

I can hear your unspoken concerns. *Will flight attendants resent this overt independence on the part of passengers?* No—although, at first, they may act surprised. In fact, as longhauls drag on, they will probably begin to show with smiles and friendly conversation that they truly appreciate one less passenger to fetch and carry for.

Doesn't self-service contradict airline marketing, which competitively boasts the desire to pamper passengers? No. These ads reveal only fluid tongues. No commercial airline I know is adequately staffed to serve each passenger the quantity of bottled water they need on board to combat in-flight dehydration.

What if everybody were to rise to the occasion at the same time? Wouldn't it cause the plane to tip over? No. Jumbo jets are not gondolas.

Bathe to re-hydrate

Bathing, when dehydrated, helps to replenish moisture right through the pores. Bathing also relaxes the nervous system from radiation, the engine vibration, and many of the other stresses you encounter when you fly. As soon as possible after jetting, submerge in water—in an ocean, a river, a pool, or a tub with a couple tablespoons of sea salt.

When checking into a hotel, request a room

with a tub, not just a shower. Let the water stand if you want to create humidity in your room. The sitting water can help humidify an air-conditioned hotel room.

After landing, urine output is one of the indicators doctors use to assess dehydration. None during the night and heavy flow in early morning is considered normal. Untimely nighttime urges to urinate can be used as a barometer of dehydration and jetlag; i.e., when untimely urges cease, you know you're over the worst of the jetlag. (Note: urinating at night because you ate or drank right before sleep is a different matter altogether.)

Post flight, it's important to remember to continue drinking a lot of water for several days for two purposes:

- To continue to re-hydrate your body.

- To assist your body to detoxify pollutants ingested during the journey.

Dehydration: Symptoms you may experience

Age lines, anxiety, bad breath, blurred vision, body aches, depression, dry cough, dry skin, headache, itching, nausea, nose bleed, red eyes, sore throat, spacey, thirsty, weakened immunity.

Therapeutic Bathing

- Close the stopper and turn on the hot water, full force. The splashing waterfall aerates and effervesces the tub with oxygen-rich bubbles.

- Add handfuls of baking soda and sea salt that you have brought with you. Check temperature. Add cold if necessary.

- Lie full length in tub. Close your eyes. Submerge. Underwater, I hold my breath for as long as I can. I'm always different after I re-surface; either my aura or my thought patterns—something changes by the total immersion. Relax in the tub for a while longer; exercise under water.

- Remain in the tub when draining water; and consciously send jetlag down and out with it. Say to your jetlag, "I send you down the drain! Adieu. Sayonara. Good bye."

- Finish with a cold shower. It is easier than you think after a hot bath. The Swedes jump in the snow after their saunas. A cold shower closes the pores.

Dehydration: Strategies for self-defense

➤On your travel day, drink one large glass of water for every hour you are in transit, e.g., from home until you arrive at your hotel.

➤Carry your own bottle of drinking water when you fly, to sip from at airports and when the in-flight service is not available.

➤On the airplane, drink bottled water rather than the tap water. Here's the scoop on the tap: there are no standards of purity for commercial aircraft water tanks—neither for cleanliness, treatment procedures, nor for water quality in cities around the world where commercial jets refill. Most airlines have mechanics fill water tanks as needed; then, to wipe out parasites and bacteria, they're told to add chlorine and bicarbonate of soda to "sanitize and sweeten" (to taste?).

➤On board, try to avoid beverages that have diuretic properties. These include coffee, tea, and all other caffeinated drinks.

➤Walk back to a galley about once an hour to combat muscle atrophy and dehydration. (Ask for a glass of bottled water.)

➤Cover your nose and mouth with a water-saturated cotton hankie. Fold the hankie on the diagonal and wrap the ends around your ears.

➤Mist your face with water every few hours. Fill a water spritzer (used for ironing and also small sizes which are sold for perfume) with your own drinking water and hold it close to your face, otherwise see the mist evaporate before it reaches you due to dryness on board.

➤Apply edible oil inside nostrils. (Almond oil smells nice. I like jojoba oil because it is a little thicker, so it is effective a little longer. Olive oil works fine, too.) Wash your hands with soap and hot water before touching inside your nose.

➤When checking into a hotel, request a room with a bathtub, not just a shower.

➤As soon as possible after jetting, submerge in water—in the ocean, a pool, or a tub—whatever is available that you enjoy. Immerse entirely, especially your head. Add baking soda and sea salt to the bath.

➤Post-flight, drink a lot of water for several days—the exact amount is relative to the weight of each individual, and, of course, to his or her diet. For example, vegetarians who eat mostly watery foods, may need to drink less water. And those who eat starchy or salty foods may want to drink more water.

Metal Fatigue

➤ *If you feel that your jet is in poor physical condition, note the details and report it.*

On July 18, 1996, the day after the TWA 800 explosion off the coast of Long Island, New York, an NBC reporter telephoned asking for assistance. *Was the crash caused by metal fatigue?* The reporter had a copy of TWA 800's maintenance log. Could I read it and tell him if there had been fuselage cracks?

I said I knew how to read the maintenance log. As a purser for many years, I had filled out logs when cabin maintenance was needed. I always checked the log when I boarded an aircraft to see if there were deferred maintenance items in the cabin that would affect our service.

We hung up, and a few minutes later thirty pages of fax came through showing the downed aircraft's maintenance history. Indeed there had been several fuselage cracks and repairs. The reporter called back, but instead of discussing this, he said he no longer needed my assistance.

Age before duty

The theory of metal fatigue was only fleetingly associated with TWA 800's explosion. Soon, the press latched on to terrorism as a theme.

Metal fatigue is determined by takeoff and landing cycles, i.e., pressurization/depressurization of the aircraft. Imagine the skin of a person who puts on a lot of weight and then takes it off—rapidly and repeatedly. The skin eventually loses elasticity as evidenced by stretch marks. Older aircraft are similarly marked with fuselage (skin) cracks (stretch marks).

Safety experts debate the limits of older jets and ways to accurately detect fuselage cracks. Some airlines buff out their fuselages instead of painting them, reasoning that cracks can hide under layers of thick exterior paint. Other airlines rotate aircraft between long-range and short-range flights, to distribute the takeoff and landing cycles, because it is these cycles which are responsible for the cracks.

After TWA 800 exploded in the sky, officials at the National Transportation Safety Board said, "What ignited the tank?...we by no means have any solid feel about how that occurred."[1] Subsequently, the NTSB and the FAA blew up another old 747 just to see if that would shed some light on the problem.

Meanwhile, it is not just the fuselage of older

aircraft that is cause for concern. The NTSB announced in March 1999 that a hydraulic valve,[2] which controls the rudder on 737's, is to blame for at least two crashes (USAir and United) where everyone died. Modifying the flawed rudder on all 737's worldwide would be costly; this is the world's most popular aircraft, and at any given moment, over eight hundred 737's are in the sky.[3]

Relatives of those who died in 737's linked to faulty rudders were pessimistic that the world's 3,330 737's would all get modified. One man, whose mother died on a 737, said in an interview that he feared the aviation industry would place business over human life and resist the costly change.[4]

The world's aging fleet is expensive. In the next couple of years, many older jets will either be cannibalized for spare parts—or the airlines will be successful in reversing aging aircraft regulations.

Metal Fatigue: Strategies for self-defense

➤If you feel that anything in your jet is in poor physical condition, 1) note the details (flight #, from/to, date, aircraft #), 2) report it (to the airline, your newspaper, your Congressperson, the FAA, the Fair Air Coalition), and 3) post it (on the Internet and on bulletin boards all over town).

Airline Policies

➤ *When calling reservations, ask if your routing includes a transit stop and/or an aircraft change.*

In addition to cutting back on oxygen, the airlines have implemented many "cost-effective" procedures in order to cut the competitive corner:

- Sardine seating.

- Shortages of airline employees at check-in counters, requiring passengers to arrive at airports several hours prior to takeoff.

- Flight cancellations at the last minute when only light loads have booked.

- Providing shoulder harnesses and smoke hoods for crew, but not for passengers.

- No meals on many short flights.

- Opening only one door after landing to disembark over 400 passengers.

- Refusing to make onward connections for passengers when flights get diverted.

Bottom line vs. lifeline

The airlines advertise quality service while they reduce the pay and increase the workload of the employees they expect to provide that service.

For crew, longer duty days and less time to sleep at layover hotels is unsafe—maybe not in an isolated incident, but certainly in the longterm. Crew fatigue is an issue the airlines will probably address only after more fatalities.

In an emergency it is the flight attendants who help passengers to safety. As safety experts, flight attendants have to memorize many different aircraft configurations with dozens of variables in equipment location and emergency procedures. Flight attendants can be assigned to work any cabin position on each of these airplanes—and each has its own safety responsibilities and equipment to be familiar with.

By way of contrast, pilots fly only one aircraft and one position (for example: a 747 captain), and they do this same job for many years. Granted, it is not the same work, but the way the system is set up now, it could likely prove fatal for some passengers.

One year, I counted over forty different cabin designs I had to memorize—some so similar they easily got mixed up in my mind. During the review prior to the FAA exam, the company instructor stamped his foot as he covered points that were to be on the exam. This was the only way I passed the recurrent training each year.

Night flights are long. Fatigue prevails. Quite frankly, many times I was so exhausted on landings I don't know what I would have done if there had been an emergency.

Sardine seating

The Boeing 757 is an absurd example of how so-called "progress" makes passengers more miserable. The aisles are narrowed to within an inch more than the cart width, so it is impossible to get by when one is in the aisle. The seats make even an average-sized person's knees butt up against the seatback in front of them. I dropped my glasses the other day on a 757, and I literally couldn't bend forward to pick them up. Luckily, the lady next to me was able to reach them for me.

The two worst features on the 757 are the lack of air blowers above the passengers' seats and the shortage of bathrooms—only four lavatories for the entire economy cabin. The 757 flight experience shoves passenger comfort many levels backwards. Although the planes of yesteryear took a longer time to get from here to there, passengers had the space to walk around and a humane amount of air to breathe.

The biggest cost-effective ploy the airlines use is called "outsourcing." This means that when an airline needs something—from maintenance to catering—they go to outside vendors. The savings come because external suppliers don't need medical coverage, vacations, and they don't get annual salary increases.

ValuJet is a perfect example. According to the press, three fourths of the people who worked on the project that caused flight 592 to burn up were outsourced, not ValuJet employees.[1] In a CBS interview, a ValuJet flight attendant characterized the airline as a sweatshop, saying employees worked past exhaustion and equipment was frequently broken.[2] Most flight attendants today—no matter what airline—privately say the same things about their companies.

Lawsuits allege ValuJet failed to maintain its planes in adequate maintenance facilities. Meanwhile, ValuJet and the major U.S. airlines plead for the government to remedy the "plight of the airlines," so they can get tax breaks, subsidies, reversal of environmental and anti-noise regulations, and cheaper labor.

What about the plight of airline passengers? It is time to speak up against an airline system that requires employees—on the ground and in flight—to take shortcuts that compromise safety. The airlines need to be regulated like the public utilities they are.

168

Hub rub

Contrary to classical geometry where the shortest distance between two points is a straight line, many airlines now practice Hub & Spoke geometry—to get from point A to point B, passengers are required to transit point C. Of course, non-stops are preferable to playing musical chairs at hubs. However, on many routes today one-stop service (not the "one stop" you necessarily want) is the only kind available, as this is most economical for the airlines.

For passengers, hub inconveniences are clear—more waiting and more flight time. Further, most of us know from playing childhood musical chairs that something is always left out when the music stops! (Checked luggage? 8% of passengers report it lost or damaged.[3] Maybe this is why 37% of frequent flyers indicate they "almost never" check luggage.[4])

Additionally, transit stops at hubs require two takeoffs and landings, as opposed to only one of each—with potentially double trouble, as most mechanical problems occur during takeoffs and landings.

Hubs also cause airport ebbs and flows as all flights arrive around the same time, congesting gateside restaurants, shops, and airline clubs. And there's the dreaded domino effect, when all connections are held for one delayed plane, everyone has to wait until all flights from outlying spokes have arrived and received service at the hub.

A late aircraft arrival is different from a rolling delay, which describes a departure that gets pushed back and back, due to a mechanical problem. In a rolling delay, sometimes you're better off trying to arrange another flight.[5]

Many passengers unintentionally end up at hubs, misled by the curious airline phrase, "direct flight." A direct flight does not necessarily proceed directly to your destination. (See explanation below.)

Airline Terminology:
nonstop/direct/connecting/through

- A **nonstop flight** does not make any stops along the way.
- A **direct flight** can pick up and drop off passengers at any number of transits along the way. This often requires deplaning, but it does not require an aircraft change.
- A **connecting flight** includes stops that require an aircraft change.
- A **through flight** involves an aircraft change, and an airline change.

Some airlines market domestic feeders with international partners, calling them "one-stop connections." Passengers get miffed. When changing airlines, they are compelled to make time-consuming, baggage-dragging terminal shifts. In Los Angeles, transiting passengers from abroad are advised to allow three hours, due to customs' backups and the circuitous path among terminals.

When calling reservations, ask, *Does my flight include a transit stop?* If it does, *Will there be an aircraft change?* If the flight numbers change, the aircraft probably changes. If the letters before the numbers change, you've probably got a terminal change.

If you miss your connecting or through flight, and it's the airline's fault, they may assume responsibility and provide accommodations and/or get you out on the next available flight but—only if your entire trip is written on one ticket. Otherwise, you may not be able to get a reservation out for hours, or even days during peak periods, and you won't have your checked luggage! Weather is the exception. It is not considered an airline responsibility.

Transit flights

When making reservations, do not book tight connections. Legal connecting time varies from twenty minutes to a couple of hours, depending on the airport and carrier. It will save you from the stress of the minor, frequent delays that all carriers encounter.

Some people go through the trouble to book illegal connections under two names because they feel transits are a waste of time. *Au contraire...*

Transits are an excellent place to recoup energy on long-distance trips. Remember: breathing and aerobic walking cuts down on jetlag. Try speed walking around the lounge for twenty minutes, then doing some stretches. Or, consider walking around to the rhythm of your own pulse.

On the bright side, when we jet in hops (up, down, up, down) instead of nonstop, we avoid higher-flying exposures to radiation and ozone.

Furthermore, flights with transit stops are not as dry. The aircraft picks up humidity each time it stops. It is really a trade off: a New York to Tokyo non-stop takes almost fourteen hours; with a transit stop in Anchorage, it's about three hours extra.

In the future, hopefully, airport designers will put the "lounge" back in transit lounges. Sleepy transit passengers, now required to disembark, find nothing but those oddly designed seats with fixed armrests and a full set of fluorescent lights. *What to do?* I just lie down on the floor when I'm tired. If I've got energy, I go off exploring.

For the undaunted, every airport is a treasure hunt. Seek and ye shall find: rooms for hire by the hour with bed and shower, restaurants featuring local food and vibes, health clubs, office centers, chapels, art galleries, and boutiques.

At Frankfurt and Narita terminals, the best shops are outside the transit areas. Without luggage, you can clear Immigration and Customs in a matter of minutes. Tell Customs, *I am in transit.* Show your boarding pass. Be sure to take your passport and ticket, too, and be apprised of local time, and your gate number. Check the monitors periodically for possible gate change. In some airports, departure gates are different from arrival ones or sometimes on a different level of the airport.

Honolulu airport has a gazebo in the middle of a carp pond—a choice spot for meditating. Follow the staircase behind the coffee shop to the lower level. Clap your hands at the edge of the pond and colorful carp come, kissing the air in expectation of food.

Climate is always something to sample when moving from place to place. One winter, transiting JFK from Hawaii to balmy Bermuda, I cleared security and adventured out into the snow.

Some airports are only fifteen minutes from a town, while others are hours away in barely negotiable traffic. Check it out with a local: If you had three hours to spare, what would you do here? Airline employees are usually open to chat when not surrounded by a crowd. Query the ones stationed at that airport, not crews in transit. Maybe you'd prefer to call a nearby airport hotel and query the concierge. Maybe you'd like to take the hotel courtesy car and use their swimming pool for an hour.

If you find yourself with five hours in Narita, Japan, for example, take a courtesy car to one of the airport hotels.

You never know what you'll discover on a transit stop. I am personally very fond of them, starting with an old transit memory. Before the non-stops from Honolulu to Sydney, we transited Pago Pago. The island folk met every flight and serenaded us while we refueled. People of all ages—the huge men in shirts and ties with wrap-around skirts; the voluptuous women draped in floral-patterned tunics, children in their arms; teenagers; toddlers—the whole community turned out. They sang their hearts out for about an hour, from 3 to 4 a.m.—then waved us goodbye.

Airport meditation

If serenity is your spring, source the meditative air in airport chapels. They are excellent places to practice positive imaging: take out your internal camera and view some films of yourself arriving safe and happy at your destination.

When you are away from your responsibilities at work and at home and you find yourself with time to spare in an airport, this is an excellent time to check-in with yourself. Amid the crowd and haste, take a moment for yourself. Sitting quietly can help you relax and become ready for a new environment where you are going—allowing you to function better.

Perhaps start by looking at the illustration on page 203. Then, close your eyes and picture this illustration in your mind. See the clock at the North Pole. See the place where all the twenty-four timezones from everywhere in the world converge.

Every time zone on Earth can be told at once—revealing the mind-boggling concept of no time at all. It's eternally NOW. True North—inside—is not a thinking place. It is a Being place. It's the Spiritual Well from which all well-being springs. It is the place from which time flies.

Airline Policies: Strategies for self-defense

➤When calling reservations ask, *Does my routing include a transit stop?* If it does ask, *Will there be an aircraft change?*

➤Transits are an excellent place to recoup energy. Stretching cuts down on jetlag. A shower does wonders. You may find a chapel where you can enjoy a meditative atmosphere.

➤If you miss your connecting or through flight and it's the airline's fault, they will most likely assume responsibility; be sure to get accommodations and connections as needed.

➤If you are a sleepy transit passenger, look for a comfortable place to stretch out, even the floor!

➤If you have an international transit, without luggage you can clear immigration and customs in a matter of minutes. Tell customs: *I am in transit.* Show your boarding pass. Be sure to take your passport and ticket, and keep apprised of local time.

➤If you are unhappy with the way you were treated on a flight, you can write the airline with your concerns. I advise people to send copies to their local newspapers, congressperson, and The Fair Air Coalition, as well. Additionally, please join The Fair Air Coalition. Through this political activism, you will combine your voice with others to make a difference. Membership information is in the back of this book.

Smoking

➤ *If you are having difficulty breathing on a smoking flight, ask for an oxygen bottle—people near you won't be permitted to smoke.*

During my flying years, smoking was permitted on all flights. I felt miserable when I worked in the smoking section, and occasionally requested the captain to turn on the no-smoking sign after dinner, before I had to pick up trays in a smoke-filled cabin.

When 60,000 ill, non-smoking flight attendants joined together to sue the tobacco companies, the U.S. Centers for Disease Control testified that a flight attendant gets the same secondhand smoke as someone living with a one pack a day smoker.[1]

The U.S. Surgeon General testified that secondhand smoke can cause heart disease, emphysema, asthma, respiratory illnesses, and lung cancer, and "the risk in an enclosed airline cabin is considerable."[2] The U.S. Environmental Protection Agency testified that secondhand smoke causes 3,000 lung cancer deaths a year to non-smokers in the U.S.[3] But the flight attendants lost the lawsuit (see pages 27-28).

Today, flights to and from the United States are all non-smoking, but many flights between airports in Asia, South America, Central America, the Middle East, and Europe still allow it. The longer the flight, the smokier the air gets because it is recycled— standing in the middle of a plane towards the end of a flight, you can't even see the last row.

On one such flight, passenger Albert Lancry slapped a flight attendant because she said he couldn't smoke while he was standing in the aisle. Lancry was sentenced to four years probation, during which time he was not permitted to "smoke a single cigarette."[4]

For the addicted, the in-flight environment definitely creates a special state of withdrawals including sweating, claustrophobia, and irritability. For this reason, when the domestic U.S. smoking ban took place in 1990, it was significant to see that nicotine-addicted pilots were exempted by the FAA because "withdrawal symptoms might pose a risk to the pilots' performance."[5]

The FAA's exemption also settled the controversy about whether or not airline pilots enjoyed separate air and purer air than the passengers and flight attendants. "The flight deck of an aircraft is better ventilated than the passenger cabin and has a separate air circulation system that does not mix with that of the cabin," said the FAA report.[6]

Passengers experiencing nicotine withdrawals often resort to arguments with flight attendants. One woman on a no-smoking flight claimed to be a terrorist and threatened to blow up the plane when she wasn't allowed to smoke.[7] Most smokers, however, probably don't even argue—they just go to the lavatory and deactivate the smoke detector by placing a shower cap or condom over it. If they get caught and the airline presses charges—which they rarely do—it could result in a $2,000 fine.

At least the air from the lavatories is not recycled back into the cabin. There is no way airlines can deliver uncontaminated air to passengers when any smoking is permitted on board,[8] reports a study done by the National Cancer Institute. Not only that, the jet environment renders this unwanted nicotine all the more toxic because cigarette smoke coupled with high-altitude air is known to inactivate a person's hemoglobin, producing temporary anemia.[9]

Doctors say the "particulate matter" from cigarette smoke is responsible for allergic rhinitis—the runny nose and sneezing some passengers suffer on smoking flights. *So why is smoking still permitted?* Certainly the airlines benefit when smoking is banned: ventilation filters and cabin interiors require less cleaning, seat selection at check-in is simplified, and the risk of in-flight fires is diminished.

The most ironic thing about the ill-fated flight attendant class action tobacco lawsuit was a statement made by the tobacco companies intending to trivialize the secondhand tobacco smoke as a cause for the flight attendants' lung cancer. The tobacco companies pointed to the in-flight ozone, cosmic radiation, and the other health risks of flying as the reasons flight attendants have lung cancer, heart disease, and more health problems than people do in other professions.[10]

Smoking: Symptoms you may experience

Burning eyes, burning skin, coughing, dizziness, headache, irritability, nervous tension, shortened attention span, shortness of breath, weakened immunity.

Smoking: Strategies for self-defense

➤If you are on a flight where people are smoking near you and this is disturbing to you, ask the flight attendant for an oxygen bottle. There is no charge for this bottle, and when oxygen is in use, no one may smoke within three rows in any direction.

➤In smoke-filled planes, breathe through a water-soaked hankie and keep your eyes closed, if possible.

Noise–and pressure affecting ears

➤ *If your ears are very painful, ask your flight attendant to notify the pilot.*

As aircraft descend, air pressure in the cabin increases. This causes our ear drums to pop. When descent is a pain in the ear, it's called aerotitis or blocked ear—an excruciating symptom often experienced by those who fly with a cold or ear infection.

To adjust your ears, yawn and harden the back of your tongue. If this remedy is too subtle, try the Valsalva maneuver: shut your mouth, hold your nostrils closed with your fingers and gently blow out.

To adjust infants' ears on ascent/descent, offer them something to suck and swallow. This works for adults, too.

On board, if you have ear pain, tell an attendant. Ask her to tell the pilots. They can repressurize manually, instead of by computer, affording more subtle adjustments. At the very least, the incident will be registered in the ship's log, so that a mechanic will check the repressurization valves after landing.

Some passengers prefer to take a decongestant to prevent blocked ears. Decongestants have side-effects, though, such as dry mouth and drowsiness—so decongestants can exacerbate jetlag.

For a few unfortunate passengers, ear problems only begin to manifest a couple of days after flying—too late to associate the problem with the flight and its rapid air pressure changes. They can use this steam-heat remedy, and it also works on board.

Steam-heat remedy to unblock ears

- Place two airline paper cocktail napkins in the bottom of a small wax-coated drinking cup—the ones found at the lavs and galley drinking water dispensers.

- Add boiling water from a galley hot-water spigot, saturating the paper napins, and then pour off the water. Be sure to drain off ALL excess water.

- Cover the blocked ear with the little cup of hot, damp paper. Pain eases in moments as the steam reaches the eustachian tube.

182

Say what?

"She must be deaf," I heard a passenger say about me on one flight, intending for me to overhear because I had forgotten to bring him something. Hearing loss, as a matter of fact, is common among crew, caused by the dual chronic stresses: rapid barometric change and noisy planes.

The mechanized air on flights can affect our ears the way a flashing light grabs the attention of our eyes. The combined sounds when flying—humming, babbling, blaring, roaring, pealing, ringing, whooshing, purring, whining, and thudding—can dazzle the brain into a peculiar stupor.

Audible levels inside jets, especially in galleys, can reach up to 96 decibels, high enough to cause permanent impairment when sustained for long periods of time.[1]

Since the advent of jets, a tremendous amount of research has been focused on noise pollution, starting with the complaints about engine noise on take-offs and landings from people living near airports. "Noise is where cigarette smoking was 30 years ago. Everybody knows it's bad for you, but a lot of people don't do anything about it."

Residents of Newark, New Jersey complained, however. Their testimony to the FAA stated that aircraft noise near a school was so severe it disrupted classes thirteen times per hour.[2] Another skirmish in the war against airport noise resulted in an award of $124 million for impaired hearing to neighbors of a military base in Japan.

On a more positive note, the environment-friendly new Munich Airport has paid to soundproof thousands of private homes near the airport. Munich Airport makes an environmental statement every day by charging landing fees up to 50% higher for older, louder planes.[3]

In 1985, the FAA enforced a ban on the noisy, first-generation passenger jets, the 707s and DC-8s. The noisy aircraft were to be modified or retired by 2000, but many airlines have applied for exemptions and received them. Many local airports want noise reductions, but the airlines are pushing for what they call "scheduling conformity," i.e., the same regulations need to be at all airports, they say, in order for them to operate effectively.

Airline employees who work on the tarmac wear ear muffs. If passengers don't want to carry bulky ear muffs, they can bring along plain sterile cotton and use a fresh piece every time, so as not to introduce any germs into their ears.

The cotton will be inconvenient at airports where we need to clearly hear announcements.

184

Once on board, consider plugging up—to muffle rather than block sound altogether. This is safe for flight, in the sense that we can still hear if emergency instructions are initiated.

A subtle-energy approach is to listen to and isolate all the various sounds on board—the engine *mmmm*, the *sshhh* as the aircraft speeds through space, the *whoosh* of the cabin air-conditioning system, voices over the PA, other passengers conversing, foreign languages spoken, even a baby crying. Listen to the subtle rhythms, too. What are the tunes of the languages? Rise above the din. Experience the cacophony as an orchestra tuning up—pick out the various instruments. Do the strings tie you to someone or somewhere?

Noise: Symptoms you may experience

Amplification of one's own voice, blood flowing from the ear, disorientation, ear pain, headache, hearing loss, impaired coordination, irritability, nervous tension, sinus pain, vertigo.

Noise: Strategies for self-defense

➤ If your ears are very painful, tell a flight attendant. The cockpit should know, as they may be able to adjust the pressure more gently.

Noise   Noise   Noise   Noise   Noise   Noise

➤If your ears are blocked, sometimes steam relieves them immediately.

➤Some headphones are designed to reduce background noise and these work well on planes. A few airlines offer them in first class.

➤Wear earplugs after the plane takes off. Don't put them in until after takeoff, so you can be sure to hear if there is an emergency on board.

➤After landing, listen to the obvious sounds of town, as well as the unheard sounds around. Take time to tune into the combined rhythms of the local social cycle. Notice the tone the cars honk, the speed the elevators rise, and the pace the people stride.

Secure for Takeoff

➤ *Always keep your eyes on your personal effects when going through airport security checkpoints.*

Air travelers worldwide must submit to body checks and X-rayed personal effects prior to every flight. After terrorists blew Pan Am's flight #103 out of the sky over Lockerbie, Scotland, in 1988, security got beefed up. But it hasn't really gotten any more affective according to experts and it has opened a Pandora's box of problems.

Today, at security bottlenecks worldwide, passengers need to be concerned about damaged personal effects—especially laptops and cameras. Kodak's high-speed film is marked "protect from X-ray," and scrambled data and broken hard drives are regularly reported by flyers. Indeed, my laptop crashed right after the one and only time I sent it though an airport X-ray machine.

Don't pack film in your luggage, either. There are even higher-powered X-ray machines for bags that go through cargo.[1]

Medications, such as insulin, are known to lose potency from airport X-rays. No one knows for sure why. It may be a knob turned too high, a security agent's too-lingering eye, or simply a cumulative effect of too many rays.

Some passengers now buy those lead-lined pouches to carry their medications, film, and data. I prefer to avoid this extra weight in my carry-on, so I ask for hand inspection. Say to security, *I know the X-ray is not supposed to ruin my film or disks or medication (because this is what they preach), but would you please do a visual check for me, anyway? I just can't take a chance with this today.*

When clearing security anywhere in the world, always keep an eye on your own personal effects. There have been a number of successful thefts of laptop computers at security points.

Here's how it works: 1) A team of thieves sees you coming with your computer case, then one of them rushes in front of you in line. The other one has already passed security is waiting for your bag to come through on the belt. 2) After you put your bag on the security belt, the person in front of you (thief #1) takes a long time with metal in his pockets or some other delay tactic. 3) Meanwhile, the accomplice (thief #2) picks up your computer from the belt and leaves.

My flight bag was stolen at LA Airport in another manner. I was waiting to check-in amidst a gaggle of flight attendants. We were in uniform, but flying as passengers to pick up our schedules. We were standing near the check-in counter while one person handled all the tickets. When I turned around, my tote bag was gone—it couldn't have been more than three feet from me.

What ensued was a trip to the police department and lengthy verbal and manual reports about the circumstances of that morning and the contents of my bag. Now, at airports, I keep my bag between my feet, on my lap or next to me with a foot or hand resting on it.

Terrorism

"Has anyone given you anything to carry and did you pack your own bag?" ask check-in agents. One asked me, "Has anyone put anything in your baggage without your knowledge?" *Well, if it was without my knowledge, how would I know?*, is, of course, the logical answer, but airline employees don't have a sense of humor about security—they are under pressure from management—so you'd better just simply say "no." Even obvious jokes about security can put you in handcuffs, like the passenger who answered the agents' question with, "I have a bomb. Only kidding." He was fined $28,000.[2]

Don't even whisper the words "bomb," "gun," or "hijack" near a check-in agent, or anywhere around security, or on an airplane.

On one flight, an off-duty flight attendant heard a passenger say the word "hijack." The man's bags were then searched, and a fishing knife and a loaded flare gun were found. The man insisted he was going fishing, and he had not said "hijack," but rather "Hi. Jack." Nevertheless, he was found guilty of carrying a dangerous weapon on an airplane—an offense with a ten-month jail term.[3]

Airports are not airtight

All this seriousness around airport security amounts to inconveniences for air travelers, invasion of privacy, and exposure to more radiation for all of us at airport checkpoints, yet the world's airports are far from airtight.

In 1999, the FAA testified before Congress with their plans for beefed up security. The FAA had gone undercover and checked five airports and found after six weeks and great expense to taxpayers that there were inadequate safeguards at airports. The FAA requested funding to check 75 more airports.[4]

Further costs to taxpayers for security are staggering. In addition to paying the FAA, explosive detection devices for 75 airports in the U.S. will cost taxpayers over $2.2 billion.[5]

Experts say that the security measures in place today are just for show anyway, and the low pay offered security personnel is a clear indicator of its low priority.

What invariably does get stopped at security checkpoints are the pocketknives and scissors of non-terrorists like you and me. Items are then tagged for baggage claim, causing more tedious delay after landing because such items are usually too small for the carousel ride. You have to claim them after landing at Lost & Found.

It's ironic, isn't it? The FAA has security personnel take away everyone's pocketknife. After take-off, the airlines give everyone a serrated knife with lunch or dinner. One way that is usually successful for getting a small pocketknife through security is to pack it along the spine of your luggage.

The flight attendant life jacket demonstration

On board, we pick up the thread of the security theme with the introduction of the life jacket demonstration, which is supposed to familiarize passengers with all the emergency equipment on board (life jackets, rafts, fire-fighting equipment, smoke detectors), as well as the airline's escape procedures in the event of an emergency.

These demonstrations neglect to provide passengers with some very important facts, such as:

- In the event of a fire, polyester clothing will melt into a person's skin.

- During a chute escape, pantyhose will cause raspberry burns on legs and fannies.

In fact, the emergency demo is usually so boring and bland, nobody watches. Passenger inattentiveness was even cited by the National Transportation Safety Board as a major crash survival problem. For example, at a Malaga crash in 1982, fifty people died in an aft cabin despite usable exits at the forward end of the plane.[6]

I urge passengers to watch the demos and to review the emergency instruction folders. In the event of a rapid decompression, we have only "18 seconds of useful consciousness" in which to pull down an oxygen mask and start breathing.

About 18 seconds before you black out is the time you have on jets cruising at 40,000 feet, experts say. At 30,000 feet, you've got about a minute, because there's a slower rate of decompression. These time periods are also, of course, relative to the physical stamina of each individual on board.

A rapid decompression is recognized by a loud bang, a rushing of air, a temperature drop, earaches, and a tornado of carry-ons.[7] Additionally, compartment doors open at each passenger's seat and oxygen masks drop within reach.

If you see oxygen masks drop, pull one to release a pin in the packing apparatus—this starts the oxygen flow.

The aircraft master tank contains only enough oxygen to keep everyone on board alive for about ten minutes! However, it is comforting to note that commercial airlines train pilots to complete a dive into what they call an "amicable altitude" in approximately three minutes.

One day, during sudden turbulence between Tokyo and Los Angeles, oxygen compartments accidentally opened and masks dropped. In unison, several hundred Japanese passengers pulled masks to their faces and, flawlessly duplicating the earlier demo choreography, turned their heads first to the left, then to the right.

Most Japanese passengers attentively watch demos, even nodding now and again to show they understand. We should all imitate them. When there are only "18 seconds of useful consciousness," there isn't time to wonder. (By the way, it's not necessary to turn your head to the left and right. Attendants display masks this way so passengers on both sides of the aisles can see.)

Securing the airplane before takeoff

Passengers are to be reminded of security at "pushback"—you'll hear an announcement that flight attendants should "prepare for takeoff." This means that the doors are shut and the emergency slides are in place. From this moment on, if a door is opened, the escape slide will automatically inflate.

Next, fight attendants come by and ask everyone to put their seats upright and stow their tray tables. This is to insure that people at the window seats can get out if there is a crash on takeoff and the plane has to be evacuated in a hurry. Securing, at this point, also includes stowing carts, compartments, carry-ons, bins, tables, and footrests. My one and only aborted takeoff convinced me of the wisdom of securing. On that day, the pilot slammed on the brakes and everything not secured on board flew fast forward.

Seatbelts must be fastened too. Once airborne, jets meet with pitch (nose up, nose down), yaw (nose up to right or left), roll (sideways), climb, sink, and speed differentials. People occasionally get sick from these motions, often with clammy skin and nausea.

Some passengers use medicated patches for motion sickness. I don't recommend them. The patches need be in place an hour prior to the turbulence; even cockpit computers can't predict this. Also, the patches dehydrate—a side-effect incompatible with jetting in a dry aircraft.

If you need to *toss your cookies*, use an airsick bag found in all seat-pockets. After turbulence, dump the contents of the bag in a toilet. Then seal up the bag in another bag and drop it in the trash receptacle in the lavatory. There are usually extra bags in the drawers in the lavatory.

At your seat, if you need an extra bag, ask other passengers for theirs, rather than ring your call button. For safety's sake, it's best for flight attendants to have their seatbelts fastened during periods of turbulence.

Although airlines request passengers to wear seatbelts "low and tight," as a general rule I believe in slack seatbelts because it's easier on the back. In the worst situations, such as the United Airlines explosive decompression of 1989, no seatbelt was adequate. Nine passengers with their seatbelts fastened flew out of the hole ripped open in the fuselage.

A slack seatbelt leaves freedom to squirm and this is easier on circulation. Be sure to fasten seatbelt outside your blanket on night flights, so in the event of turbulence while you sleep, attendants will leave you in peace. Waking people to fasten their seatbelts is part of the overall flight attendants' responsibility as mandated by the FAA. Towards this end, a highly technical annual training has been designed.

The review includes familiarity with oxygen use; dry chemical, halon, CO_2, and water-based fire extinguishers; inflatable vests and rafts; and transmitters for rescue. We are taught that even airsick bags can be enlisted as emergency equipment. For example, to activate the aircraft's sonar beacon after crashing in a desert, we are instructed to urinate, neatly, into an airsick bag, then submerge the sonar beacon in the urine. After fifteen minutes, supposedly, the water-soluble tape dissolves, releasing a whip antenna which then transmits the aircraft's bearing 26 miles omni-directionally, with an operating life of 48 hours.

The flight attendants' annual emergency review also covers hyperventilation, mouth-to-mouth resuscitation, cardiac arrest, bleeding, burns, in-flight death, food poisoning, hijackers, delivering babies, and evacuating by land or sea. By land, we are told to slide down a chute and flee. By sea, we are supposed to assemble with the passengers on the chutes themselves, then unzip from the mothership, and *voila*, a raft for about fifty folks.

We are reminded to hurry. Why? First, a ditched jumbo jet is predicted to float for only fifty minutes. And second, "in most serious crashes, 50% of the ten available exits on 747s fail to work."[8]

Finally, an announcement over the PA instructs flight attendants to be seated. This final announcement before takeoff is made by the captain or co-pilot. It tells the flight attendants that the aircraft is ready for takeoff—that in a moment or two the airplane will start racing down the runway.

Secure for Takeoff: Strategies for self-defense

➤Bring a photo ID to the airport, something to identify yourself to the ticket agent. Most airlines will not accept checked luggage without a photo ID.

➤Advice from a security expert: "Ordinary passengers can help by quietly informing security staff if they see anything suspicious, on public transport to and from the airport, at the airport, and on airplanes. Better to feel a fool for ten minutes than be dead twenty-five years early."[9]

➤Always keep an eye on your personal effects at airports (especially security) and on board airplanes.

➤Don't even whisper the words "hold up," "hijack" or "bomb" at an airport or on an airplane.

➤Arrive early at the airport to avoid stress at security checkpoints, especially if you have something that needs hand inspection. If you want your laptop, camera, film, medications, snacks, or vitamins hand inspected, instead of putting them through the X-ray machine, take time to offer a smile to security guards.

➤Put your coins, nail clippers, and key chain in your briefcase, instead of in your pocket, before you enter security. You will clear the metal detectors without needing to empty your pockets.

➤To expedite hand inspection of film, remove the film from the cardboard boxes when you pack and put each roll into a clear canister (used by some brands). Put all the film in a clear plastic bag.

➤If you don't want a hassle at airport security with your pocketknife or scissors, try packing them along the spine of your luggage.

➤Wear natural fiber clothing for your flight—it will protect you better if you have to escape down an airplane slide, or if there is a fire on board.

➤Be sure to fasten your seatbelt outside your blanket on night flights, so in the event of turbulence while you sleep, attendants will leave you in peace.

➤If you see oxygen masks drop, you need to pull one toward you to start the flow of oxygen.

Symptom Chart–Air travel risks & remedies

Does flying leave you with swollen feet, depression, nausea, coughing or insomnia? Turn the page for a chart showing you the health hazards caused by flying. Proven remedies and detailed descriptions of the symptoms for these hazards are found in the chapters which are named along the left-hand side of the chart. For example, if your eyes are swollen, red or infected, look down the column "Eye Problems" and then across to the chapter names on the left that offer remedies and strategies, such as "Air Quality" and "Dehydration." In these chapters, you'll find out why your eyes are red or infected and what you can do about this before, during, and after your flight.

The outlined airplanes indicate a number of hazards that could cause moderately dangerous symptoms. The solid black airplanes indicate extremely dangerous hazards that could cause symptoms requiring medical attention.

Symptoms Caused by Flying

Flying Hazards (Chapter Titles)	Bloating	Body aches	Coughing	Depression	Digestion	Ear Problems	Eye Problems
Air Quality	✈	✈	✈	✈	✈		✈
Dehydration	✈	✈	✈	✈	✈	✈	✈
EMF				✈	✈	✈	
High Altitude	✈	✈	✈	✈	✈		✈
Noise				✈		✈	
North/South		✈		✈	✈		
Ozone			✈				✈
Pesticide	✈	✈	✈	✈	✈	✈	✈
Radiation				✈	✈	✈	
Smoking			✈	✈			✈
Stress		✈		✈	✈	✈	✈
Time Zones		✈		✈	✈		
Toxic Chemical	✈	✈	✈	✈	✈	✈	✈

🛩 = *Dangerous* ✈ = *Extremely Dangerous*

Proven remedies and more detailed descriptions of the symptoms can be found in the chapters named along the left-hand side of the chart.

Legend: D = Dangerous, XD = Extremely Dangerous

Fatigue	Flu	Feet Swell	Headache	Insomnia	Nausea	Nervous	Poisoning	Rage	Spacey
D	D		D			D	D	XD	D
D	D		D	D		D		D	D
D	D		D	D	XD	D			D
D		D	D		D	D		D	D
D			D	D		D		D	D
D				D	D	D			D
D			D			D		D	D
D	XD		D	D		D	XD	XD	
D	D		D	D	XD	D			D
D	D		D		D	D	D		D
D			D	D		D		D	D
D			D	XD		D			D
D	XD		XD	D	D	D	XD	XD	D

Facing the Dragon

As you get to know the dragon, you realize you don't need weapons to fend it off. Shine a light into the dragon's den— the light of self-awareness will protect you and help you to avoid injuries. Self-awareness comes from paying attention—through taking care. Defensive remedies are all about taking care. Learn what not to eat on board, how to sleep in an economy seat, how light affects metabolism, and about body-work. Be open to esoteric exercises too.

Defensive Flying—good advice even if you are not flying

In this world with swelling population and increasing pollution, we are exposed to many contaminants in daily living. So stepping into in-flight contaminated environments should give us an incentive to take as many precautions as we can.

For frequent flyers with mileage awards of mega-jetlag (see "Mega-Jetlag"), a normal routine just isn't enough to help us stay healthy and be our best while flying. We have to work at it.

But if a passenger flies only now and again and the flight isn't very long, he or she may not feel much jetlag (and thus may not be inspired to practice defensive flying).

How quickly do you want to bounce back from jetlag and how much does flying drain you of energy and clear thinking? This section offers dozens of strategies—both practical and esoteric—for healthy living as well as healthy flying.

Light Therapy

➤ *If you're tired, but have to work, turn up the light.*

Light is effective for modifying metabolism. Speeding up metabolism with light has actually been used for centuries to make songbirds sing in winter when they are normally silent. Today, poultry farms have bright artificial lights to make the chickens lay more eggs. But hens sometimes peck each other to death under bright lights in crowded conditions.[1]

And then there was light

Some airline passengers hope that light therapy will solve all their problems associated with jetlag. Light *can* speed up and slow down the sleep cycle, but, of course, light does not address the low air pressure, pesticides, and other environmental hazards on board the aircraft.

Although light therapy is widely advertised as a remedy for jetlag, today, reasearchers, unfortunately, disagree on how to apply the light, leaving travelers in the dark—or pecking at the closest moving object.

Some of the most popular recommendations for light therapy actually conflict with each other. These publicized theories I find unproductive for passengers. One scientist insists you go outdoors when it's sunrise-time back home.[2] Another says take three hours of bright light for three days but warns that morning light can increase jetlag.[3] A third counsels us to use morning light only after flying east.[4]

One significant aspect of light as it relates to air travelers is not mentioned by these theorists. The unusually long daylight periods passengers experience on westbound longhauls speeds up metabolism. For example, the flight from New York to Tokyo departs around noon and lands fourteen hours later with bright daylight streaming in aircraft windows the whole way. The natural light en route is more brilliant and energizing above the clouds than anything that filters down to us on earth. I have found this to be especially so when it reflects off glaciers on polar routes. (I flew 300 polar flights—roundtrip.)

Passengers are exposed to different amounts and intensities of light, but the cure for all light imbalances is the same. After flying, spend time outside in natural light. Both sunshine and moonlight will put you in harmony with local rhythms and cycles.

Light management for air travelers

• Spend some time outdoors every day. Even being in a room with windows during daylight enlightens our body clocks. The larger the windows, the quicker the adjustment.

• Winter: fly from the tropics to a higher latitude, a place such as New York—the shorter day-to-night ratio in New York slows down our metabolism.

• Winter: fly to the tropics from the higher latitudes—light in the tropics is so bright that it energizes our hormones.

• After landing, as you step outside the terminal, take time to feel your senses shift from your former geographical world to your new environment. Give your cells the maximum opportunity to begin acclimatization though sampling and discerning, with heightened awareness through all your senses, the new meteorology.

Tune in to light as it fluctuates in your immediate environment. Give yourself more light according to your own energy requirements. You can do this by simply turning on a light, screwing in a brighter bulb, or going outside in the middle of the day when, for example, you are tired and need energy. Sunlight or bright indoor lights literally quicken my pulse. For relaxation or sleep, candlelight or filtered light through curtains or blinds also works just fine.

Remember: after jetting, don't stay inside all day away from natural light. Outdoor light, at any time of day, automatically cues our cells.

Did you know that our bodies secrete adrenaline an hour before sunrise? We don't even need to be awake or watch a sunrise for this to take place. It happens every day before sunrise and is the Creator's way, a biological chip, if you will, to help us get up in the morning.

After changing time zones, this adrenal secretion is out of sync for a number of days while it homes-in again on the local Sun cycle. Although we don't have to be outside at sunrise to re-set this cycle, watching a sunrise truly helps. Being awake early in the morning also helps a lot. It's as if doses of energy are given out in the mornings and you have to be vertical to receive them.

212

Wake up

Some scientists maintain that human beings can only input environmental light through the eyes, suggesting that we are less adaptable than birds or lizards which perceive light in other ways. It is this writer's judgment that these scientists are wearing blinders. Many times I feel sunrises before seeing them. For example, during the decades when I was pirouetting around the planet, I became a fan of sunrises and sunsets as seen from the spectacular vantage points of jets. I was surprised when my inner clock started cueing me. Even in the middle of a busy service—I'd get that certain feeling to glance out a porthole, just in sync with a sunrise. On layovers, too, even behind an eye-mask and blackout curtains, regardless of what time zone I was in, or how much sleep I'd missed, I'd often awaken, uncannily alert, in tune with a sunrise.

I've witnessed countless heavenly light shows around the globe, even a couple green flashes—those emerald-light bursts a second before a sunrise and also a second after a sunset as the Sun comes up or goes down on the ocean. We all have this subtle sensitivity within reach.

Have you never set an internal wake-up call without an alarm clock?

Entering a cold climate

Temperature differentials between departure and arrival locales can shock the system of even the most seasoned flyer. For example, every winter, some residents from Hawaii (a humid, hot spot) rush to Colorado (a dry, cold spot) to ski. And movie moguls migrate back and forth between Palm Springs (a dry, hot location) and London (a humid, cold location).

My formula for the climate shift from hot to cold entails confronting the first bite of cold air head on, with these three steps:

> 1) I go into the airplane bathroom and put on my silk long underwear. Silk (for women and men) is lightweight and packable.

> 2) In the bathroom, I rub a deep-heating lotion (over-the-counter) on my chest, on my kidney area, and on the soles of my feet.

> 3) After touchdown, I take 100 milligrams of natural niacin (Vitamin B3). Soon, I'm feeling warm all over. This lasts long enough to transition out of an airport and into a hotel.

Every location has a unique microclimate created from the local humidity, temperature, altitude, wind, ion count, and pollution—all simmered with natural geology and man-made technology.

Light Therapy: Symptoms you may experience

Body aches, circulation problems, coordination problems, headache, rage, recklessness, tension.

Light Therapy: Strategies for self-defense

➤Dress in layers when you travel so you can adjust yourself to the temperature changes pre-flight, in flight, and after landing. Your carry-on should include a sweater, socks, and hat or scarf, especially if you are flying from a hot climate to a cold one. Aircraft, by their very design, are warm in some areas and drafty in others. There is no way to accommodate all passengers on any flight with their individual temperature comfort zones.

➤Wear your heaviest shoes on board, so you don't have to pack them. Additionally, the aircraft floor, especially around the toilet areas and galleys, is usually puddled.

➤When you first enter a cold climate, stay warm with deep-heating lotion and silk long underwear.

➤After landing, as you step outside the terminal, take time to feel your senses shift from your former world to your new environment. Be aware of your body's needs and address them.

➤For at least three days after flying, spend as much time as possible outside during daylight hours or, at the very least, in a room with windows.

➤Tune in to light as it fluctuates in the environment from moment to moment. If you are tired, give yourself light (natural, if possible). If you want to sleep, withhold bright light.

➤Wherever you are, enjoy sunrises and sunsets. Join me in watching for the green flash.

Sleep

➤ *Sleep at night at your new destination.
Force yourself, if necessary.*

The most immediate and intimate problem faced by passengers after flying across time zones is missed sleep and sleep cycles that are out of whack.

Statistics show that most car accidents occur when we would normally be asleep, between midnight and 2 a.m.[1] Business travelers who have to work when it is their bedtime at home are prone to accidents, too—maybe their figures collide with someone else's at the negotiating table.

Sleep deprivation can touch our well-being on every level, even where we may notice it least— emotionally. MIT researchers reported that even though their subjects claimed to be unaffected, symptoms (in particular, irritability) became apparent beginning twenty-four hours after the period of missed sleep.[2]

Night flying for pilots has been found to impact the safety of passengers.[3]

As an international flight attendant, I missed sleep about ten nights every month. When I didn't get enough sleep, my body would occasionally nod off (without my permission). Many nights, I actually fell asleep sitting upright on those rigid airplane jumpseats. So much for safety.

As a matter of fact, on a couple of night flights, I found all three pilots asleep at the controls (during cruise, not landing). No doubt their bodies nodded off without their permission, too.

The pilots' seats are more comfortable than passengers' seats. In addition to recline, they have lumbar supports, adjustable armrests, adjustable thigh supports, and shoulder harnesses to keep them from slumping over if they fall asleep.

Sleeping at night is something most of us take for granted at home, where we function a lot on automatic pilot. After jetting, however, we need to take responsibility for re-setting our sleep cycles. This can be done simply by sleeping at night.

Adjustment of your sleep cycle may take up to a week. And bubbles of drowsiness may surface on the third or fourth day after flying as the second wave of jetlag catches up with you. However, this second wave is only a small swell to quell if you've had the will to force yourself to sleep at night.

Sleeping pills

Some passengers take sleeping pills as soon as they get on board. They zonk out after takeoff and doze away flight tedium. Even President Bush used pills for long flights;[4] that was until reporters started suggesting that some of his strange speech patterns, such as referring to the Nitty Gritty Dirt Band as the "Nitty Ditty Nitty Gritty Great Bird,"[5] may have been caused by sleeping pills.

On another continent, Boris Yeltsin's aides publicly stated that their boss' slurred speech during a U.S. visit was not due to drinking bouts but sleeping pills he had taken for jetlag.[6]

If these heads of state are having trouble handling sleeping pills when they travel, what about us normal folk without a staff of aides to watch over us?

How do we manage if there is an emergency on board and we're under the pall of sleeping pills? One flight attendant, who was working when her aircraft ripped open at 24,000 feet (4-88), recalled: "I was collecting empty glasses when, suddenly, a thunderous blast knocked me out of my shoes. A passenger helped hold me to the floor."[7] Thank God this passenger hadn't taken sleeping pills!

If you think about the fact that every flight could end in an emergency, passengers are best served by staying alert and not taking drugs on board.

Even without such dramatic close encounters, sleeping pills, when used in conjunction with jetlag, are known to have a side effect of short-term memory loss.[8] Imagine not having the capacity to retain information just received, such as directions to your hotel or other essential services, when traveling in foreign destinations.

Of course, each passenger will deal with sleep problems as she or he chooses. I do not endorse the use of sleeping pills for airline passengers.

Melatonin

Melatonin is advertised as the jetlag wonder cure. The initial announcement, however, included some shocking side effects, such as "melatonin is a possible inhibitor of sexual development in rats."[9]

Subsequent research brought forward more warnings about melatonin. Taken at the wrong time of day, or in the wrong amounts, it could actually worsen jetlag with side effects of depression, headaches, and constriction of the arteries to the heart.[10] For a complete list of side effects, please tune in ten years from now. Not all the data is in, and those who regularly use melatonin will be part of the statistics.

I found that the day after I took melatonin,

there was a thickness and slowness about my thinking, as if the neurotransmitters weren't firing properly—creating a veil of stupor over my mind all day.

I am skeptical of melatonin touted as a jetlag drug, an anti-aging drug, and an estrogen replacement drug. We're all starting to realize that we can't trick our bodies with anesthetizing chemicals forever. Somewhere consequences will be paid.

There is no sleeping pill, natural or synthetic, that cures jetlag because jetlag is caused by more than just lack of sleep. Jetlag is actually a multitude of environmental challenges that we can't neutralize with just one little pill. No pill can fend off the pesticides and radiation on board, but a sleeping pill or sedative can exacerbate some aspects of jetlag, including fatigue.

Rather than taking a pill, I prefer to eat, then soak in a very hot bath right before going to sleep. This is how I managed to sleep on demand, no matter how jetlagged I was after thousands of flights.

Pillow talk

Eileen Ford, the duenna of the prestigious Ford Model Agency, travels first class around the world several times each year in search of more "perfect" faces like Christie Brinkley. When Ms. Ford stated with perfect frankness, "You could hit me over the head with a hammer and I still wouldn't sleep on a plane,"[11] she articulated the sentiments of many.

On the other hand, when Marlon Brando was my passenger on a night flight between Los Angeles and Papeete, he managed to sleep all flight through—as though he had been knocked on the head with a hammer. After dinner, Mr. Brando pulled out the center armrest of his first-class seat and fixed a bed for his young son. Then the star fell asleep on the floor, where his feet would normally be.

He slept soundly until landing, his legs stretched across the aisle of our aircraft. I couldn't bring myself to tell him he was in violation of a FAA Regulation "impeding access to the exits." Instead, all night I stepped over him as I served other passengers—each time wondering if Marlon Brando would glance up.

How to sleep in an economy seat

Often on longhauls when the economy section is sparsely populated, first-class passengers come back to claim a row of seats. Although fully horizontal seating has recently been introduced on some airlines in first class, seats on the majority of carriers don't get fully horizontal.

222

I've found that such posture actually cramps my ability to drop into the kind of deep sleep I am able to access when I'm lucky enough to score a whole row of seats in the back. I suspect this is because hormone rhythms are posture-dependent.[12] You have to be horizontal for deep sleep.

Ideally, we would always travel during the day, then fall into restorative slumber in a real bed at night. Red-eye specials, however, are cheaper than daytime fares. The night traveler also saves the price of a hotel room.

On night flights, many passengers nod off draped over armrests, as limp as empty garment bags. I remember two men, one awake, the other asleep on his seatmate's shoulder. I was serving soft drinks from a large tray. As the first man took his, I suggested, "Would you like to take an extra for your friend when he wakes up?" His response: "I have never met this man before." Yet, he didn't wake the stranger who found comfort on his shoulder.

For some passengers, sleeping upright in an airplane seat is impossible. It used to be for me, too. However, now I've had so much practice—during breaks when working longhauls and as a passenger taking advantage of my travel pass privileges. My technique for sleeping in an economy airplane seat involves a certain investment in preparation.

Props for sleeping on an airplane

- Drinking water
- Sterile cotton for ears
- Eye-mask
- Handkerchief
- Oil (edible) for nostrils and skin
- Neck pillow
- Socks
- Sweater
- Tooth brush

If you've been unable to sleep in jets, I'm sure you'll also find this investment worthwhile, especially on red-eyes eastbound when it helps so much to get at least a little sleep on board, because you don't want to sleep in the morning after arrival.

Here's what works for me.

Boarding

1) If you're scouting a place to stretch out, check armrests before claiming a row. Usually, front rows of each section have armrests that don't pull out or stow up. Also, in front of emergency-exit rows, the seats don't recline.

2) Stow your carry-on, and find a pillow and a blanket. Check the overhead bin nearest you for pillow and blanket. If it's empty, you can check other bins. They are not assigned. You can claim one pillow and

one blanket from anywhere in your class. Economy passengers attempting to take a cloth-covered pillow or a large-sized blanket from business class or first class will be chastised. If you do not find a pillow and blanket, ask attendants. There is usually a stash.

Prior to takeoff

1) Nibble a snack, so you won't be tempted to eat the airline meal. Swaddle yourself with a sweater, socks, and an airline blanket for cocoon-like privacy. Fasten your seatbelt loosely outside the blanket so it's easier to turn from side to side. Flight attendants, seeing the belt fastened, won't wake you if the seatbelt sign comes on.

2) Wet a cotton hankie with your own drinking water. Cover your nose with the hankie to stop the spread of germs—the flu and TB. The wet hankie also creates humidity for your lungs.

Takeoff

1) Recline your seat as the aircraft wheels leave the runway. The upright position is required for taxi and takeoff only, in the event of an emergency.

2) Place the airline pillow behind your head. Cradle your neck in an inflatable pillow. Don an eye-mask.

3) Tell your subconscious: *Wake me when the plane starts to descend.* Your cue will be a lower engine whine.

4) Doze off with the g-forces on ascent. If you wake up early due to dryness, wet your hankie again, and resume deep sleep. For me, this works every time.

Top of descent

Wake up. Get up. Use the lavatory. They are usually empty until the landing announcements are made, about fifteen minutes after descent begins. Splash cold water on your face directly from the faucet, not the sink bowl. Wash your hands with soap and hot water. Reapply oil to your nostrils. Circuit the plane for exercise. Return to your seat. Sip water.

Getting in step

It's always beneficial—physiologically, fiscally, and socially—to sleep when it's night locally. Accordingly, adjust your bedtime to the local timetable as soon as possible after landing. Otherwise, pay the price of nighttime insomnia and/or daytime inertia.

Resist going straight to bed after a night flight. Sleeping in the morning will definitely prolong your jetlag. There are two reasons. First, when you sleep during the day, you are usually not tired enough to

Review: How to sleep on a jet

- Ask for a window seat, so you have a wall to lean against.

- Wear an eye mask to help you stay asleep.

- Swaddle yourself in a cocoon with airline blanket, pillow, sweater, shawl, and socks.

- Attach a note to your eye mask with masking tape that says, "do not disturb" so attendants won't wake you with offerings.

- Fasten your seatbelt outside of the blanket so attendants won't wake you during turbulence.

- Keep a bottle of drinking water handy to sip from during periodic awakenings. It's so dry in the aircraft cabin that the body wakes up in alarm at the dryness.

- Moisten a cotton handkerchief with your drinking water and place it over your nose to prevent your sinuses from drying out.

- Dab edible oil, such as olive or jojoba, inside your nostrils to keep the delicate membranes from cracking.

sleep again that night. Second, **if you sleep in daylight during the first twenty-four hours in a new time zone, you're actually notifying your cells that you want them to ascribe to a daytime sleep cycle. Cells reset themselves while we sleep during the first couple of days after arrival in the new zone.**

For awhile, our cells can act befuddled at new bedtimes because they're used to being sleepy at a certain time. The new bedtime feels like the wrong time. It's as if our cells are trying to listen to two pieces of music at the same time. The old time zone's melody is fading out, but it's familiar. Meanwhile, the new song of the new time zone begins to dominate the subtle energies.

After long-distance flights, we must face the music. The best, quickest, most efficient way to do this without drugs is to go to sleep at the local bedtime. Don't waste any effort on trying to alter your bedtime prior to leaving home. Why inflict additional traumatic sleep adjustments on yourself unnecessarily? After landing, the Almighty Law Of Time Zones automatically assists us—so go when the force is with you. Travelers should ignore the once popular theory that you "stay on home time while abroad," with one exception.

Exception: Crew and frequent flyers on turnarounds of less than 48 hours should stay on home time or no time. These trips are, literally, too quick to bother adjusting. It's better to go with the flow—sleep when you can, and eat when you feel like it.

How to fall asleep after arrival

Many passengers can't fall asleep the first night after arrival, particularly after eastbound flights when night appears to arrive too soon. My routine for falling asleep, any time I want to, is as follows:

1) I eat a high-carbohydrate meal.

2) I take a long, hot bath in semi-darkness, by candlelight or with the bathroom light out and the bedroom door ajar—just so there is very soft light. I add baking soda and sea salt or Epsom salts. I soak as long as possible with my head under water.

3) When I get out of the bath, I go right to bed. The bedroom is made as dark as possible with curtains and blinds. I also close off all windows of my body with eye-mask and earplugs. I lie down comfortably under the covers and pull them up over my mouth.

4) I imagine I am outside my body. I see my body asleep, as if from the other side of the room. Then, I send my awareness into the sleeping form. As my imagination merges with my perception, I am asleep. *It's one of my best tricks.*

Sleep Deprivation: Symptoms you may experience

Anxiety, body aches, confusion, constipation, depression, fatigue, fear, headache, impaired vision, indecisiveness, insomnia, loss of coordination, low blood sugar, muscle stiffness, nausea, nervous tension, poor vision, rage, restlessness, sleepiness, sore throat, weakened immunity.

Sleep Deprivation: Strategies for self-defense

➤Don't alter sleep patterns before leaving home. You'll need that precious rest to ready yourself for the travel experience.

➤To regulate your sleep cycle in flight:

- • Sleep on board, if you land in the a.m.
- • Don't sleep en route, if you land in the p.m.

➤On turnarounds of less than 48 hours, keep your sleep cycle either on home time or no time, rather than attempt to adjust it in any way.

➤Wet your handkerchief and cover your nose and mouth with it for personal humidity.

➤As soon as you get on board, find a pillow and blanket in an overhead bin near your seat. If there aren't any, ask any flight attendant.

➤If you want to change seats and you're looking to stretch out across two or three seats, remember that the front rows of each section usually don't have moveable armrests. Also, seat backs in front of emergency-exit rows generally don't recline.

➤Fasten your seatbelt outside your blanket on night flights, so in the event of turbulence while you sleep, attendants will leave you in peace. Also, wear a sleep mask with "Do not disturb" written on it.

➤Create a soothing cocoon to nurture deep rest. Use the airline blanket and pillow along with some props you've brought along —a sweater and socks, eye-shades, sterile cotton for your ears.

➤On descent, it is best to be awake in order to consciously adjust your ears.

➤Adjust your bedtime to the local timetable. Sleep at night at your new destination.

➤To prepare for sleep, darken your hotel room and take a long hot bath.

➤Avoid artificial sleep aids, such as sleeping pills and melatonin; otherwise, expect artificial results and possibly dangerous side effects.

➤If there is anything you are concerned about which may keep you from really resting, such as, *Are my valuables safe?*, take care of it or let it go.

➤ For help with balancing the emotions, I've found a flower essence available at health food stores by the name of "Rescue" is an excellent travel aid. I mix a few drops in my own bottle of water, and regularly sip from it en route. This makes a tremendous difference in the way I feel and react.

Bodywork

> ➤ *A facial or foot massage actually stimulates all the organs of the body.*

Nothing can equal the power of touch to discharge tension built up from flying—whether that touch comes from a friend, a loved one, or a professional bodyworker.

Ironically, touch can even dissipate the tension of trying *not to touch or be touched* by other passengers when we fly. After charging the crowds at the curb and the legions in the lines, we cram into narrow seats, elbow for space on the armrest, lobby for legroom, and hope not to be kicked in the seatback or bumped by carry-ons. Being attentive to your poise in a populous world is of benefit to you and everyone else on board.

Be attentive to the energy pathways in your body. This is an often-neglected journey to the near reaches of the body/spirit borderlands. Make your connections and explore this territory when you travel. You'll be pleased by the results.

Our bodies have invisible rivers in which energy flows through us. The Chinese call this energy "chi," the Hawaiians "mana," the Hindus "prana."

When the current flows unimpeded, all flourishes on the banks (our organs). If there are dams (areas of tension), floods result above (flu), or it becomes parched below (constipation).

Energy blocks caused by tension, toxins and jetlag are released through bodywork—so are endorphins, the feel-good hormones.

On a subtle level, the touch of someone who's grounded in a new time zone can help to ease our jetlag. After landing, passengers met and embraced by family and friends have a head start. And who doesn't appreciate a hand with the luggage?

Bodywork: Symptoms indicating you may need it

Anger, anxiety, depression, fatigue, headache, muscle stiffness, nervous tension.

Bodywork: Strategies for self-defense

➤You can do bodywork on yourself. A facial or foot massage actually stimulates all the organs thanks to the energy pathways that run throughout the body.

In flight, massage your feet and calves. Find tender places and hard tight places. Take deep breaths while you work on them. Apply pressure for a minute; then release and apply again until the tenderness subsides. What about seatmates' reactions? Would you dare to offer him or her a foot massage or shoulder rub? I can see the headline now: FLY THE TOUCHY-FEELY SKIES—STRANGERS TRADING BODYWORK ON JETS.

➤Once in your hotel room, massage your body with an edible oil, such as jojoba, to combat jet-induced dry skin. The oil penetrates easily after a hot bath and can work all night if you apply it before sleep.

➤Also, for jet dryness, drink a half teaspoonful of unpesticided, cold-pressed olive oil first thing in the morning for several days after flying.

➤After flight, try skin brushing. In France, friction gloves are sold for this. They look like pot holders and feel like pot scrubbers (not steel wool ones, of course). A vigorous, full-body rub takes about sixty seconds. For best results, brush before showering. Brush daily when you brush your teeth. When flying, brush often. After a few weeks, regular brushing imparts a glow to the skin. The body's electrical fields have been turned up—a powerful force against accumulating any tension. May the Powerful Force against accumulating anything be with you!

Diet

➤ *Skip the meal on board. If you can fast on your travel day, that's the best strategy.*

If you put kerosene into your car, you cannot expect it to run properly. If you eat junk food, you cannot expect your body to perform optimally.

Diet is especially critical when you fly because of the tremendous added stress imposed on your body from all the environmental factors in the airplane.

Although many areas of the travel ordeal are beyond our control, what you eat on board and on your entire travel day is totally within your control. If you decide to skip the meal, your whole travel experience will improve as a result of this one simple action. I urge you to try fasting when you fly. Just skip the in-flight meal, and then eat after landing, picking up the new, local mealtime.

As for the in-flight service, there really is not anything I would recommend eating on commercial jets. The airline services I've seen are typically high in fat, full of sugar and salt, chemically processed, bland with pasty sauces, and lacking wholesome complex carbohydrates.

Airline companies advertise gourmet fare, especially in first class, but the truth is, eating an eleven-course meal of any quality will leave you, after landing, with swollen intestines full of undigested *excess baggage*.

It's the low air pressure on board that makes our bodies swell up like the Michelin Tire man—and with expanded intestines, it's tremendously difficult to digest any food.

The choice is an individual one: 1) arrive hungry, then eat after landing, or 2) eat an airline meal, then spend an extra week struggling with the body's demands for food at odd hours.

Pie in the sky

Airline meals are not healthfully prepared. They are precooked on the ground, frozen, and then reheated on board in aluminum pans.

Most airline meals are cold by the time they're served to passengers. Malfunctioning equipment on board (ovens and carts) is common on most carriers. The low air pressure makes foods get cold faster as well. But still, people say it's hard to skip the meal. They are tempted even when they're not hungry!

238

Airline meals *do* pass the time, but it's a false sense of marking time—not synchronized with the mealtime at either your departure or arrival city.

So, in this sense, eating at odd hours on the airplane actually interferes with the resetting of all your internal cycles that are associated with digestion and assimilation.

On the other hand, **eating at the local meal time after landing helps to jump start the digestive cycle to the new local time zone, through stimulation of what scientists call "food triggers" and "social interaction ticklers."**

If you can, it's best to skip all solid food between your departure location and your arrival destination. After landing, eat a meal on local time. In other words, if you land mid-morning, eat lunch when the local people are eating lunch.

Want to eat on board?

If it is not appropriate for you to fast on the airplane, bring along some snacks made from high carbohydrates.

Mountain climbers claim that a pure carbohydrate diet gives them an "altitude advantage" of 2,000 feet. Climbers know that a pure carbohydrate diet enables them to function on less oxygen.[2]

Since the interior altitude of a commercial jet is as high as a mountain resort, i.e., 8,000 feet above sea level, it is definitely considered a low-oxygen environment. So any altitude advantage for airline passengers is extremely helpful, making us feel better and function more effectively.

On a high-carbohydrate diet, I've sustained energy over long periods—like a horse, and as a flight attendant I certainly worked like one!

On a subtle energy level, when we address our bodies' nutritional needs, we automatically provide ourselves with wholesome food for thought.

Supplements on board

If you intend to eat on board, you may want to bring along a mineral supplement to take with every meal. The minerals in our bodies, so necessary for healthful functioning of our physiology, easily get depleted when we're dehydrated on board.

When I fly, I also like to take extra doses of vitamin C every couple of hours between meals (buffered, time-released, 1000-6000 mg. per 24 hours).

While fasting, it's best to skip intensive supplementation because of the shock to an empty gastrointestinal track. Remember: it's important to drink a lot of water the whole time you are on board.

Fasting or not, there are two herbs that I take to support me when I fly—echinacea and noni. These two herbs are available in capsules, in tinctures, and as teas. Echinacea has antiviral properties so it is certainly efficacious as we are exposed to many viruses in commercial jet cabins.

The herb, noni, is not as well known, but I highly recommend it for travelers to help with detoxification after flying and to build up the immune system. As a matter of fact, I am so impressed by noni—I feel it saved my life when I stopped flying—that I wrote a book about it (*NONI–Aspirin of the Ancients*, published in 1998).

How to order a special meal

Many passengers believe that by ordering special meals, they will get better quality food. Special meals are still frozen dinners cooked in aluminum pans.

The biggest problem with a special meal is that you cannot count on it being delivered to the flight. If you want a special meal, you can't pick up the airphone and call for a pizza, although this would certainly seem possible with the advancement of today's technology. If you really want a special meal, you need to keep reminding the airlines about it.

Here's what you need to do—your best shot for getting a special meal delivered to your seat on board your flight.

1) When you make your reservation, request your special meal. Ask for a confirmation number (the "record locator number").

2) Reconfirm your special meal with Reservations about 48 hours before your departure.

3) At the check-in counter ask, *Is my special meal in the computer?*

4) When boarding, give a note to the flight attendant in your section—with your name, seat number, and the special meal requested.

And, yes, special meals do make extra work for flight attendants. But putting your request in writing will definitely make it easier for them and probably quicker for you. Depending on where the meal is stowed, you may be served later or earlier than the rest of the passengers in your section.

On most airlines, a variety of special meals are available. Some are specific to certain sectors, such as Japanese meals on flights to Japan and also to Brazil where there are many Japanese residents.

Most special meals are available on all sectors and can only be ordered for flights where meals are served.

Special meal options

- Vegetarian—no meat, fish or eggs.

- Hindu—spicy, Indian-style vegetarian.

- Kosher—the cutlery and plates have never been used, and the meat is slaughtered, and served according to Kosher law.

- Moslem—no pork.

- Japanese—sometimes served on fancy lacquerware.

- Child's Plate—often a hamburger.

- Fruit Plate—it's usually fresh; you can ask flight attendants to leave on the plastic wrap so you can nibble on the fruit when you feel like it.

- Seafood—usually a choice between cold seafood salad or hot seafood entree.

- The Prescription Diets—Diabetic, Gluten-Free, Bland, Soft, Low Calorie, Low Carbohydrate, Low Sodium, Low Cholesterol/Fat, and Sulfite-Free.

Meal choices

When there is a choice of meals, don't count on getting your choice, even in first class. Here's how you might go about getting what you want from flight attendants: court them as you would anyone else you might woo for favors. Dinners, golf games, and envelopes stuffed with $100 bills are, of course, not appropriate in the airways. Any small gift, something practical and of low weight and low volume, such as a silk scarf (or a copy of *JET SMARTER*), is always appreciated. In addition, it is important to acknowledge that you are asking for an extra service. In today's bottom-line economy, with provisioning and labor reserves spread thin, it is impossible for flight attendants to give everyone on board what they want.

The airlines are aware that some passengers on every flight will not get their meal preferences. This inequity is ignored. There was a time, so long ago that it is now classified as airline mythology, when crew meals were provisioned from the first-class stockpiles to insure that every first-class passenger, at least, got his or her preference.

From a healthy flying point of view, you might consider the bent of your intestines over the zeal of your palette. Remember that in the low air pressure on board, our guts are swollen, rendering first-class meals as hard to digest as economy fare. Possibly you could look at things another way if you don't get your meal choice. Let the others in the front rows eat cake. You are flying smart class and that means you don't necessarily care to eat at high altitude. You can enjoy a meal of locally-grown food after landing.

Eating is such a personal thing. It serves many functions. It's a form of energy. It's social. It reminds us of our childhood. It's a substitute for sex. Therefore, I suggest that you do your own food thing when you fly while using your best informed judgement and tuning in to your bodily needs, flow, etc.

Diet: Symptoms caused by food problems

Bloating, depression, digestive disorders, headache, illogical food cravings, low blood sugar, low energy, modified reactions to drugs, muscle spasms, nausea, nervous tension, poor concentration, rage, spaciness.

Diet: Strategies for self-defense

➤If you intend to eat on board, you may want to bring along a mineral supplement.

➤Two herbs that air travelers may want to take are echinacea and noni. If eating, take between meals. If fasting, take any time.

➤If possible, refrain entirely from eating during your flight. Drink lots of liquids en route, and after arrival, enjoy a meal (of local foods when available) at the appropriate mealtime at your destination.

➤The interior altitude of a commercial jet is as high as a mountain resort, 8,000 feet above sea level. You will get an "altitude advantage" if you avoid protein foods on board.

➤If it's inappropriate for you to fast, pack carbohydrate snacks in case you get hungry on board, and in case of airport delays. Ethnic restaurants, such as Thai, Chinese, Lebanese, and Indian, all have high-carbo meals to go—vegetables with pasta, rice, millet, or couscous, etc. Health food stores also have takeout sections with high-carbo selections. In a pinch, you can grab a bag of pretzels or rice cakes.

➤When deciding if you want to skip the in-flight meal and snack on carbohydrates, or only drink liquids (fast) on your travel day, consider:
  • Hour of departure.
  • Duration of the flight.
  • Room in your carry-on.
  • Advice from your physician.
  • Restrictions of agriculture and Customs.

246

Exercise

➤ *Stretch during the flight—whenever you can—and always stretch right before sleep.*

Stretching helps us to recover from jetlag. Flexibility triggers emotional stability and it also helps us physically.

To be most effective as a jetlag remedy, stretching should be done right before sleep, but on board as well, whenever possible.

After some hours in the air, passengers often feel like zoo animals in too-small cages—fed, dull, but agitated. Indeed, the longer the flight time, the greater is your need for stretching and exercising.

Although the space at your seat is extremely limited, exercise is possible on airplanes. This chapter suggests many exercises that you can do, even in economy class! Included are physical, mental, emotional, and spiritual exercises—a comprehensive package for jet travelers.

I hope you don't worry about looking silly to your seatmates. Rather, know that you are taking care of you. Others will believe what they want to—and maybe they will join in.

Of course, it's smart to consult a physician before starting new exercises. (I have to say this.) Progress at your own pace. Perhaps do a few exercises across a time zone or two. Or, do a few and then stop to snack, or take a nap. You'll definitely avoid discomfort later.

Let your body lead the way

While in your seat, slowly contract, then release every muscle you can think of. Tense, then let go, isolating every muscle in any progression you choose—your feet, your legs, your perineum (see my book on yoga for detailed information about the power of the perineum), your stomach, your chest, your arms, your neck, your face.

My father used to wiggle his ears to entertain me when I was little. I'm thinking of him now, suggesting that you activate all your body parts sequentially and in isolation. You may find you suddenly have an urge to raise your knees, alternating right/ left to a count of ten. Possibly, your wrists or ankles want to turn like pinwheels. Or, your arms feel like reaching for the sky—*inhale, exhale*—for the benefit of your lungs. You can stretch your fingers and toes. I'm sure your own body will let you know.

Get up and circuit the plane

Get up and walk around the cabin every hour to stimulate your blood circulation. There are serious consequences to sitting without moving for many hours in pressurized airplanes. One is called Economy Class Syndrome, also known as Quayle Syndrome, referring to the thrombophlebitis (blood clot) suffered by Vice President Dan Quayle while flying.

When the flight attendants and carts are not blocking the aisles, be smart—get out of your seat and promenade, ramble, march. Or, walk like Groucho with straight back and slightly bent knees. This loping stride pumps even more blood up to the brain.

The Groucho walk is also easier on the knees as the jet's thin aluminum flooring has a trampoline effect. Notice the floor's angle; jets fly nose up to save on fuel.

While circuiting your jet, feel free to peruse galley centers. Here, find hot-water spigots for making your own herbal tea or instant soup whenever you want a non-caffeinated warm drink. Ask a flight attendant, when she or he is not busy, to brief you on spigot etiquette.

Other highlights on your tour may include magazines, which are stowed on both sides of bulkhead partitions, and telephones when they're not located by your seat.

Keep a lookout for fire extinguishers and portable oxygen bottles, kept in appropriately labeled overhead bins, or in sideways compartments near the floor behind the last row of each section.

In any event, it's fun just to check out a one billion dollar vehicle. Yes, each 777 costs one billion dollars.

Visualizations

We often start our flights with the best intentions to read a good book we've brought along. But how many of us land and haven't read that book at all? One of the reasons for this is that it is difficult to concentrate in a low-oxygen environment.

Visualizing, however, does not require the same kind of focus reading does, and lends itself easily to high altitudes. Visualizations have been found to affect physiology even at a microbiological level. And visualizations are known to improve performance in sports and in business.

From your seat on the airplane, you can visually transport yourself anywhere—away from the crowded, contaminated cabin into a clean, spacious place.

The most powerful visualizations are personally created, but here are some samples to get you started.

250

Visualization #1. Close your eyes and travel to a place in your mind where the air is crystal clear. For instance, see yourself walking on an autumn morning. Stride along a winding, sun-dappled pathway. Sunlight gleams through a montage of colorful leaves on trees. Hear the leaves crackling underfoot. Take in a breath every time you need to. *Inhale. Exhale.* Let the breath out every time you need to.

Visualization #2. You prefer jogging? Sprint along a wide sandy beach. Inhale. Hear ocean waves crash and lap at your feet. *Exhale. Inhale.*

Visualization #3. Dive into the pale green water. It is warm and silky. Iridescent sparkles dazzle each little crest. Swim out from the shore. *Inhale. Exhale.* Stretch with confident, powerful strokes. Hear little splashes as your hands slice through the water.

Visualization #4. You have a preference for frozen water? Go skiing. It's that perfect powder morning. The air is crisp blue-white. Snow flies by your face as you slalom effortlessly downhill.

Float freely to pleasant places in your mind's eye. Remain internally light, not too serious, like the wafer-thin cirrus clouds outside, matching feelings to the awesomeness of higher altitudes.

Then, with the next incoming breath, open your eyes and smile.

Send E(nergetic)-mail

Create a picture in your mind of a message you want to send someone down on Earth. See it in vivid color. Hear it spoken in your mind. Then, condense it into a little ball of light. Zip it up and zap it on its way. See it received and acknowledged.

After arrival, ask the person to whom you transmitted, *what happened at such and such time?* Maybe she or he thought of you then, and fixed up the guestroom. Check it out. Some day we might discover that telepathy works best from jets, where we can operate like satellites.

Soaring scenery

Enjoy—really enjoy—the view outside at high altitudes. Do not be intimidated by anyone who suggests you must close your porthole shade; it is never required. However, if glare prevents the sleep of others, you might consider partially lowering it or trading seats with someone on the shady side of the plane.

I have witnessed many glorious natural phenomena from portholes of jets—an active volcano, the Aurora Borealis, glaciers, mountains, atolls, clouds of all shapes and sizes, circular rainbows, numerous breathtaking sunrises and sunsets, and the lights of a Japanese fishing fleet which looked like an out of place constellation of stars.

Enthusiasm for the view—or anything for that matter—speeds up jetlag recovery time. How? When we are enthusiastic at what we see, consciousness is pulled along into the present, automatically. When we enjoy what we are doing while we are doing it, it makes the *now* present, and truly a gift—that's why we call it the present.

Circular rainbows

Three times I've seen circular rainbows from jets—perfect concentric circles as if drawn with a giant compass. The first time, arriving in New Zealand early one morning, I saw double—two circular rainbows—one inside the other. The inner circle had red on the outside and purple in the center, like a normal rainbow. The larger circle was reversed, and paler.

Years later, somewhere over Asia, I saw another pair of rings. More relaxed this time, I watched them disappear when there were no clouds below, and reappear as clouds presented backdrops for their colors.

I saw my third set flying in a small jet one stormy day between islands in Hawaii. Again, the colors were only visible with clouds below. And, now, with the clouds quite close, in the middle of the rings I saw the shadow of our jet.

Refracted sunset

At sunset, seven suns are refracted on the double-ply porthole plastic. Yellow to orange to red, the suns slip behind a horizontal cloud envelope— and get mailed away beyond the horizon.

Perfect pyramid

Hilly green below is marked with darker patches of trees, meandering rivers, small villages of modern day Mayans, and then a sprawling metropolis consumes the spaciousness of an entire verdant valley.

We are floating above Guatemala. Now we pass through a blue cellophane bag of sterile cottonball clouds. Below us is a volcano, a perfect pyramid.

As I glide directly over its top my questions are answered magically and I know what it is I wanted to know.

Freedom isn't just flying free. It's being able to perch with a singing heart like a bird in a cage with no bars and no door.

Porthole viewing—one step further

Aspecting is porthole viewing taken into the next dimension. Aspecting from jet portholes is an exotic way to get to know yourself from inside out.

The principle of aspecting is that whatever we perceive most in our environment stands out to us because it is a reflection of what we're feeling, wanting, or processing.

Here's an example of aspecting. Today as I was starting my yoga practice, I looked at the sky and the cloud that caught my eye resembled a giant fork.

What could this mean, I asked myself. *Oh, I want to eat* immediately popped into my mind. So I addressed the part of me that would prefer eating to exercise, *Yes dear, we'll have a nice breakfast after yoga.*

Aspecting is a pleasant and easy way to create a bridge to the subconscious mind. It's especially easy with clouds, and the portholes of jets the perfect place to get started.

We can address worries not known to us before. And we can ask the subconscious for help. For instance, *What does this mean?* we might ask, if we see an aspect we don't understand.

The answer may come in an intuitive flash, as mine did about the fork in the clouds and eating.

Trust yourself to have answers and look for them through this new window to your *self*—this porthole of the mind. Hear what your heart has been saying all along.

Affirmations

Affirmations are helpful for the many stresses of air travel, even including fear of flying. Here are two affirmations appropriate for air travelers:

- *I count my Blessings and do my best. I trust that the Almighty Pilot takes care of the rest.*

- *All the living cells of my body work in perfect harmony. I am well (and how!), and clearly present in the here and now.*

Terminus tune-up

When you've arrived at your destination, get physical. Play tennis, swim, a jog, dance, lift weights. Go for whatever is available and what you enjoy most.

Walking in Nature is an antidote to jetlag. City parks, botanical gardens, and zoos are places to roam when we're away from home—assisting travelers to revive and to acclimatize. Long walks after landing oxygenate the blood while the cells soak up local light and color in a new time zone.

Exercise: Symptoms indicating you may need it

Anxiety, back pain, depression, digestive disorders, disorientation, headache, impatience, joint pain, muscle stiffness, neck pain, nervous tension.

Exercise   Exercise   Exercise   Exercise   Exercise   Exercise

Exercise: Strategies for self-defense

➤Don't be embarrassed to exercise. Walk around the aisles with your knees bent, like Groucho. That position stimulates blood flow and brings oxygen to the brain.

➤Air travel is like a mileage marathon. Grueling trips to airports dragging and lifting luggage, long treks in terminals *schlepping* carry-ons, rushing and contorting, once on board, to stow carry-ons. After landing, rushing, contorting, retrieving carry-ons in haste, dragging them out jetways, or up down flights of stairs, heaving them on and off customs counters, and lugging them, again, in and out of ground transportation. Like an athlete, train yourself for the airport trek. Close your suitcases a few days before departure. Try them around the house for size and weight, even practice lifting your carry-on, as you would lift it into one of those overhead storage bins, about six feet high.

➤Enjoy the view out the porthole of your jet to speed up jetlag recovery time.

➤Walking in Nature is an antidote for jetlag.

➤Stretching helps us to recover from jetlag. Flexibility coexists with emotional stability. Stretch on board and right before bed.

Taming the Dragon

 *Now you have mastery over the dragon! Practice your mastery of flying in the chapters "Fear of Flying" and "Stress." Fly better than you've ever flown before. Test yourself with "Flyana's Exam." There's more to learn, and it could be fun. Soar upon wings of experience and discovery. Enjoy flying. Learn about the postage stamps featuring air travel—enjoy the stamps for pure artistry and gain a new perspective for history. Take the Laggin' Dragon for a ride. Have fun.*

Fearless Flyer

> ➤ *Repeat after me: "I like to fly. I'm at home in the sky."*

Is flying more dangerous than driving? Yes. **Flying is more dangerous than driving,** although statistics created with insufficient data would have us believe just the opposite. Statistics on loss of life from flying do not take into account, for example, the man who died of lung failure in a Sydney hospital after getting sprayed with pesticide, nor the infant who died after her flight across the Atlantic.

And, there are no statistics on loss of *quality of life* from flying, such as the saga of the young Japanese translator who had been flying around the world assisting CEO's. One day in business class, the contents of an overhead bin tumbled out in turbulence. A suitcase knocked her unconscious. The airline refused compensation, even refused to give her the name of the passenger whose bag it was that hit her on the head. She is now in constant pain, unable to resume her work due to impaired memory.

So why do we fly? For the most part, the airlines reliably get us from point A to point B. It's faster than driving, and sometimes even costs less when you factor in overnights at hotels. We fly when we need to get from here to there for business or family reasons. We fly when we need a vacation. Worldwide, more than one billion of us fly each year. U.S. commercial carriers reported an operating profit of $9.2 billion dollars in 1998.[1]

I live on an island, and I definitely prefer the airplane to a ship. The airplane has only five hours of aviation-fuel smelling air—a ship will have five days of diesel-smelly air.

Not liking air travel is different than fear of flying. I receive more letters about fear of flying than any other subject. Here is an excerpt from one of them which shows some unique reasons for not flying: "I have had a fear of flying most of my life. I always fear that the plane will crash. I have been more frightened since the TWA crash for several reasons. First, the date of it, July 17th, is the birthday of my late uncle, so I already associate death with that date. Second, 800 was the same flight I took twelve years earlier as a student going to France. But most significant, there was a French teacher with her students on that flight, and I am now a French teacher."

Common reasons for fear of flying include

overworked controllers, weather, and runway crashes.

Controllers—they are overworked and under-staffed. During the seven minutes prior to a runway crash at LAX (2-91), the controller had handled fifteen planes!

Weather—some conditions cause fatal accidents. Wind shear (upside-down tornadoes) and wind rotor (sideways tornadoes) have claimed many lives.

Runway crashes—in Chicago (4-99), a cargo plane barely missed a passenger jet with 300 people on board when one of the pilots made a wrong turn on the runway.[2] Runway near-misses occur one in every thirteen thousand flights; twice that many planes take off from Chicago's O'Hare Airport every month.[3]

What would you guess is the biggest cause of airline accidents today? Experts say it is "human error" causing 66% of all airline accidents.[4] Possibly the most serious example of human error comes from the annals of the now-bankrupt Eastern Airlines. Over a four-year period, mechanics intentionally installed defective gauges that allowed unsafe planes to fly.

A Detroit runway collision (12-90) was blamed on four sets of human errors: 1) controllers, 2) airport designers, 3) tailcone release device, and 4) pilots.[5] Is it human error when a fatigued pilot crashes at a congested airport in bad weather? To err is human. And to be human means one day to face death.

Choose to be a fearless flyer

Personally, I believe in fate and Divine Law. I always have. There is no room for fear of flying in my belief system because my very purpose on Earth is part of a continuum where I'm working toward intrinsic qualities—developing perseverance and compassion—that will endure with me past death.

I can understand how a person, lacking some steadying belief system could become gripped by fear of flying. Sometimes I work with fearful flyers on the telephone and many of them, I've found, are ambiguous about what they think happens after they die. Most tell me they have avoided these thoughts and, when pressed, they describe death as "just turning out the light," or "it's just over."

Thus, fear of flying seems to me, at its essential core, to be fear of dying. Even Mohammed Ali in his heyday admitted this. "The only thing in the world I'm scared of is flying," he said in an interview on TV. "I imagine the plane splitting in two, and me falling into the ocean, and then the sharks biting me!"

Many famous people admit they are afraid to fly—Whoopi Goldberg, Aretha Franklin, John Madden, and Isaac Isamov are some of the most well-known. The rich and the famous get to enjoy the bounty of our world more than most of us do, so it makes sense that they'd resist leaving it more, too.

The press says Cher is afraid to fly. One night, she boarded my flight looking like plain Jane. I would not have recognized her if the ground agents hadn't told us that the celebrity singer was coming on board. Cher looked tired; she took her first-class seat and clearly told me: "No food. No drink. No conversation." Then she closed her eyes and slept for the entire flight without even reclining her seat. I figured she'd taken some sleeping medication.

The innovative Stanley Kubrick, the American film director of "2001," "Spartacus," "Dr. Strangelove," and "Eyes Wide Shut" didn't leave England for the last 31 years of his life—he was simply too afraid to get on an airplane, it was reported.

I heard this from Dan Bloom, a journalist living in Asia and a famous fearful flyer himself. When Dan Bloom's visa expired in Japan, he faced criminal prosecution and even went to jail rather than get on an airplane.[6]

Have faith

If fear of dying is at the root of your fear of flying, do yourself a favor and examine your belief system. Speak to your minister, take up meditation, go to the library. Investigate death while you are alive.

Many people who come through near-death experiences go on to live richer lives. They say in facing death, the secret of life is revealed. Remember that United jet that crashed in an Iowa cornfield (7-89)? 110 people died, but 186 survived! This was attributed, in part, to local rescue efforts. The whole town responded in moments. Two doctors were available for every hospitalized patient. Neighbors waited in line for hours just to donate blood.

Uncannily, two years prior to that accident, this town had actually run through a drill in which a jumbo jet was assumed to have crashed nearby and 150 survivors needed immediate help.[7]

This kind of coincidence bolsters my faith. How does it affect you?

One survivor said, "When you come through something like this, you feel like you have time you didn't think you would have, so you look at everything as being a little more valuable."[8]

Perhaps you could choose to look at fear of flying as an opportunity to see differently.

Cold feet

"Ladies and gentlemen," I said to a full first-class cabin one morning, "I have something to tell you." All passengers suddenly grayed. *Engine trouble?*

Fearless Flyer   Fearless Flyer   Fearless Flyer   Fearless Flyer

I hadn't meant to distress anyone. I was simply in a hurry. So I quickly resumed, "Sorry to startle you. There's nothing to worry about. We have no knives and forks on board, that's what I need to tell you. No cutlery was provisioned today. Do you still want us to serve dinner?"

Passengers, relieved that there was no trouble with the plane, immediately began to connect with each other with smiles and conversations.

One woman with a toddler held up a bag of plastic forks, "Will these help?"

Applause and cheers followed like team spirit in a locker room.

The flight turned out to be one of the most pleasant of my career. It's true! Friendliness makes flying easier and more fun.[9]

Similarly, on another flight, Sammy Davis, Jr. boarded at London's Heathrow with smiles and kind words for everyone on board. He cracked jokes and truly entertained us for 13 hours to Los Angeles.

Even when we ran short of fuel on that flight, and made an unscheduled stop in Newfoundland, standing on the snowy tarmac with Sammy became a fun thing to do for everyone on board, even the captain.

It was one of the easiest flights I've worked. Friendliness helped us all to feel our best.

JET SMARTER by Diana Fairechild   **269**

Fear of flying: Symptoms you may experience

Anxiety, inability to concentrate, jaw clenching, nervous tension, panic attacks, shallow breathing.

Fearless flyer: strategies for self-defense

➤Enjoy yourself. Rather than allow your mind to become snagged in a fear of flying mental loop, concentrate on the fun you plan to have after landing.

➤Feel prepared for an on-board emergency:

> 1) Understand your oxygen mask—*if you see an oxygen mask drop, pull it toward you.*

> 2) Know how to get off the airplane even in the dark—*count the rows from your seat to the two closest exits in opposite directions, in case one exit is blocked or disabled.*

➤Be friendly and kind to other passengers and to airline employees. Worldwide, the airlines employ about a half a million people.

➤For more information about Fearless Flyer Consulting: Reliable Strategies for the Aeronautically Challenged, log on to "Healthy Flying" on the Internet: <www.flyana.com/ff.html>.

Customs

> ➤ *To expedite Customs clearance, smile and lean towards the inspector with friendly body language.*

The word "customs" in this chapter refers to Customs agents at airports who search through airline passengers' personal effects, and also to local customs—the rites and rituals of everyday life which are different in each place around the world.

In Japan, for example, people are quite fanatical about cleanliness, to the point that Customs agents at the airport invariably wave a person on with a white-gloved hand, rather than look through a bag that has dirty laundry on top.

Waiting at Customs or Baggage Claim always includes an element of stress. *Did my bag make it?* If it did not, airline liability for luggage lost on an international flight is only $635. If your bag is lost, you have to file your claim before leaving the airport; then later prove your claim with receipts. The airlines will depreciate the value of your things rather than replace them.

Always pack layover essentials in your carry-on, just in case your bag is lost or stolen. Include your prescriptions, travel documents, money, and valuables.

Tact or friction

Arriving in a foreign land can be disorientating, especially coming to a place where you don't know the language and you can't even read a street sign.

Think of how many extra maneuvers you have to go through in a foreign country just to get a good meal. Some of the most obvious extra steps are changing money, getting the name of a good restaurant, studying a city map, translating a menu, and adjusting to unfamiliar tastes.

Travel requires that we adjust ourselves according to the local customs—the hours that people work, and how long they take for lunch are customs which vary from place to place. We also need to be aware of body language—a nonverbal communication.

Cultural symbols

One example of body language is how people greet each other from country to country. Do they bow, shake hands, or kiss?[1]

In every culture there is specific body that is used as shortcuts for common word "yes" and "no." For instance, Japanese people are not accustomed to saying "no" directly. Instead, they use a gesture which looks like waving one hand in front of the mouth. I saw this on hundreds of flights, and it took me a while to catch on. If a Japanese passenger didn't want another cup of coffee, he would wave his hand in front of his mouth to mean "no." If he wanted more coffee, he would simply point to his cup.

In India, when people want to gesture "no," they raise their chins. This is a gesture that usually means "yes" in the west, so, it's confusing to westerners. But the most confounding body language in India is when people say "yes" by shaking their heads right to left to right while smiling.

One spring evening in New Delhi, I was invited by some local people to attend an opulent wedding. A huge mansion was festooned with flowers and populated with bejeweled guests. To the blaring of trumpets, the bridegroom, wearing a gold breastplate, rode in on a white horse.

Many servants graciously offered delicious food heaped on silver platters. "Don't you notice?" my host pointed out. "See, they are only offering potatoes."

I hadn't noticed. Who could imagine that only potatoes were served at a fancy wedding?

The Potato Eaters took on a whole new meaning during Indira Gandhi's first term with its "austerity measures," one of which forbade hosts at large gatherings to serve anything but potatoes! Luckily Indian cuisine offers a wide variety of choices—*pakoras* (deep-fried); kebab (marinated and grilled); *bhaji* (with mustard seeds, coriander, and coconut); *dum* (with yogurt, ginger, cloves, and cinnamon); song (with tamarind); and *paratha* (mashed inside a sandwich).

When I think of India, my mouth starts to water. Ironically, people from India can go hungry in the West due to misunderstandings of local customs. For example, an Indian friend told me that when he visited California, he nearly starved! At meal times his hosts asked him, "Are you hungry?" and out of politeness he would say, "No," despite his hunger. "In India," he explained to me, "unless a host tries to coax you to eat, it is not polite to accept."

Local customs around the world are rapidly disappearing like endangered species. Over the years, as I've moved around the planet, I've kept an eye on the world's progressing homogenization as an ongrowing current of events. Multinational corporations are almost everywhere now, replacing local customs with polyester uniformity.

Focus on what you want

For many years, I traveled with a camera to record local customs. Photography offers a helpful analogy for travelers. When taking a picture, we can keep what's not important to us out of focus simply by using a close-up lens or a shallow depth of field.

In the same way, when we focus on the positive—when love fills the heart—the journey becomes both a means and an end.

Customs: Strategies for self-defense

➤Put your name and phone number on the inside of each piece of luggage. Remove old tags.

➤Pack layover essentials in your carry-on in case your luggage is lost or your flight gets delayed. Include prescriptions, travel documents, money, valuables, water, sweater, socks, scarf, hankie, toiletries, oil for inside the nose, and snacks. Under-pack: it is less tiring and less expensive.

➤Make a list of your personal effects while you are packing. It is easier than trying to reconstruct a list at the airport Lost & Found counter if your bag is lost.

➤Airline rules and prices can literally change by the minute. Deals are available if you are flexible.

➤Worldwide, customs agents tune into body language in order to separate travelers with symptoms of jetlag from smugglers *with intentions which zigzag*. To expedite customs clearance anywhere, display friendly body language; smile and lean towards your agent.

➤If you don't want your bag examined in Japan, just sneeze over it as the agent approaches you!

➤If you are new to the eyes and minds of the people of your destination land, your best strategy for alleviating cultural chasms is to open up with childlike curiosity.

Stress

> ➤ *Before flying, check with your doctor regarding your health care needs (pregnancy, cardiovascular, etc.), and to adjust your prescribed medication dosage and timing.*

In probing the subject of jet stress, we meet the final dragon in this text—Aviation Super Stress (the ASS dragon).

Travelers either harness this monster and ride it, or they are adversely affected by it with back problems, headaches, and glitches in the gastrointestinal tract. Those possessed by ASS are soon consumed and, hence, become asses to all and sundry.

Harnessed ASS (HA) results in a powerful state of health and well-being. One remains balanced, while functioning effectively in the immediate reality of the moment.

We have seen how an air traveler's health—physical, mental, emotional, and spiritual—is compromised by jet travel. This also works in reverse—how we choose to adjust to the multiple stresses of jetlag and the in-flight environment will affect our journey at every stage and on every level.

Here's a little test. Picture yourself accomplishing the following air travel tasks—and as you observe yourself, imagine you can actually feel your level of stress. See this stress in your mind's eye on a scale from 1 to 10. And then neutralize it—detach from the drama and balance yourself within.

How good are you at staying in neutral in stressful situations? What are you like as you research airfares, or make decisions on hotels and transportation at your destination?

Is packing and handling baggage a struggle or a juggle? Do you like to leave your house a certain way or in disarray? Take care of mail? Your auto? Last will and testament?

At the airport, how do you greet the agent? Do you face delay with equanimity? Bristle at security?

How is it on the runway, waiting for a takeoff slot with no circulating air?

Eating and sleeping off schedule? Exploring new ways of being? Are you smiling or sulking?

When we jet, we need to be prepared to meet stress, for stress has never been, nor will it ever be, denied a boarding pass. And the best way to meet stress is with your internal security mechanism fully engaged. And the best way to make sure it is? Pay attention to how you feel.

Soaring

As we taxi the runways of our normal daily life—moving here and there to make way for others, advancing into place towards our goals—we find, that it is often stress (lack of money, unrequited love, even illness), which empowers us to soar.

In aviation, aircraft engineers deliberately introduce stress into an aircraft's flexing skeleton to create tenacity beyond the potential strength of individual parts. Humans too are endowed with tenacity beyond our apparent strength. Time and again we prove fit to carry whatever weight is placed upon us—even literally.

For example, on takeoff we must sustain an increased G-force (gravity weight).

On the ground we all weigh 1 G. On ascent, we weigh between 1.5 and 3 G, depending on the aircraft's speed and its angle of climb. With 3.0 G's, for instance, a person weighing in at 125 pounds on Earth, will momentarily feel the massiveness of 375 pounds. But we adapt so naturally we hardly notice it.

Maximum human tolerance is defined as 5 G for 5 seconds, when blood pools in legs, and hearts are incapable of pumping enough blood back up to feed the brain with oxygen. The result is first loss of vision, then loss of consciousness—unless you're wearing one of those special G-suits designed for fighter pilots.

On commercial jets, as increased G's thrust us backwards against our seats, our blood also tends to pool a little in the legs, resulting in a slightly decreased flow of oxygen to the brain.

Aerodynamic attitude

Increased G's on takeoff is the easiest time all flight to fall asleep if you've got your pillow and blanket ready. Though it only lasts a minute and can be so negligible that we usually ignore it, g-forces on takeoff can also serve as a turning point towards metaphysical thought.

Try this on for size: *how much we feel we weigh is an opportunity to change our perceptions.* For example, a loss of fifty pounds is usually accompanied by a transformative personality shift. Or, going in the other direction, when a slight person suddenly weighs 375 pounds, even for a moment, she or he can use this magnification to see *through form*—into what is generally invisible and unavailable.

Take advantage of the turning points of all your takeoffs. As aircraft climb, we have a few precious moments to jettison everything that no longer serves us, even old ways of thinking—our excess baggage from the past in the form of guilt and fear dissolving along with the dark smoke that your jet spews.

The force of G

The letter G has so many meanings in the English language. It's an abbreviation for "Good" in grading and for "General audience" in motion picture ratings. It's a musical key, a thousand dollars, and a pleasure point in tantric sex. Gee whiz!

As with all things, there are so many ways to look at it. In the end, the choice is simply up to us. Every moment we have another opportunity to re-set our intentions, to remember to choose happiness.

Like an airplane, the body can fly high or fly low. When we travel in commercial jets, it is up to us to determine what kind of journey we have. We can race through airports, bristle at delays, down cocktails (later regretted) while en route, arrive with swollen guts, toss and turn that night, nod off at meetings, misdirect anger, and blame it all on jetlag.

Or, we can deliberately employ jetlag as a tension-loaded springboard, and feel better for it. We can choose to tame that Laggin' Dragon—jetlag.

Stress: Strategies for self-defense

➤Prevent stress from stowing away on your journey. Pay your internal security mechanism its fair wage by paying attention to how you feel.

➤Increased G's on takeoff is a light-headed opportunity to fly through the inner door to dream time.

➤Takeoff is the easiest time all flight to fall asleep, if you're ready.

➤On takeoff, if you want to immediately stimulate your blood circulation, massage your calves.

➤As the aircraft climbs on takeoff, mentally jettison everything that no longer serves you, along with the dark smoke your jet spews.

Flyana's Exam
—earning your wings

Part I. Multiple Choice

1)   Alternate names for jetlag are:
      A.   Cabotage.
      B.   Circadian desynchronization.
      C.   Dysrhythmia.
      D.   Dimwits' Disease.

2)   Non-stop flights from New York to Tokyo:
      A.   When we include the ground time driving to/from airports, may take twenty-four hours.
      B.   Do not have smoke-free zones because Japanese people, in general, love to smoke.
      C.   Are the longest nonstops in the world.
      D.   Arrive at an airport out in the boonies.

3)   Airlines don't permit these people to sit near exits:
    A.   Deaf passengers.
    B.   Most Samoan passengers.
    C.   Handcuffed prisoners accompanied by armed guards.
    D.   Elizabeth Taylor.

4)   The "best" seat on a jet is:
    A.   Near a lavatory.
    B.   By a window.
    C.   On an aisle.
    D.   Next to Elizabeth Taylor.

5)   Airline policy regarding traveling with a pet:
    A.   Only one cat, dog, or bird is permitted in each aircraft cabin.
    B.   Pets must remain in closed, sealed containers throughout flights.
    C.   A seeing-eye dog is not considered a pet; it may accompany a blind passenger without additional charge.
    D.   Seeing-eye dogs are too large to ride in commercial jet cabins and must fly below deck in cargo holds.

6)   Airline policy regarding children:
    A.   Children five years old may travel alone on nonstop flights.
    B.   Children under two must be held whenever the seatbelt sign is on.
    C.   Children under eleven always get a 20% discount.
    D.   Children flying alone may never sit in first class.

7)   The "English muffin standard" is:
    A.   A first-class breakfast service on flights to London.
    B.   A flight attendants' test for food doneness.
    C.   A controller's term for ruffled low clouds.
    D.   A standard term for radiation exposure.

8)   The word "embarkation" defines the following:
    A.   Receiving a boarding pass.
    B.   Everything which takes place between arriving at an airport and boarding.
    C.   Going to ARRIVALS to depart because you've just arrived at the airport.
    D.   Being chased by a pack of dogs.

9) In flight, each first class passenger:

    A.   Has his or her own emergency exit.

    B.   Enjoys three times more air than economy travelers.

    C.   Gets to visit the cockpit.

    D.   Is rich and/or famous.

10) Changing seats in flight enables one to:

    A.   Sleep lying down across several seats.

    B.   Get the best seat in the "house" for the movie.

    C.   Receive a meal sooner.

    D.   Receive a second meal.

11) On jets, we may operate these devices:

    A.   Handheld computer games.

    B.   Cellular phones.

    C.   Remote-controlled toys.

    D.   Vibrators.

12) The first movie ever shown in flight was:

    A.   High and Mighty with John Wayne.

    B.   Introduced by SAFE Airlines.

    C.   Introduced in the sixties.

    D.   A silent film introduced in the 30's, which was perfect because headsets hadn't been invented yet.

13) If you feel nausea and dizziness two hours after landing, the cause could be:
   A. Perilymph fistula.
   B. A flu caught on board.
   C. Food poisoning.
   D. Culture shock.

14) To "complete a dive" in airline jargon means:
   A. To fly to a tropical locale and learn to snorkel.
   B. In flight, to suddenly lose altitude, then level off.
   C. To be under a drip from the ceiling in the main cabin caused by a leaky upper-deck lav.
   D. To frequent bars where airline pilots hang out.

15) Stewardesses were first introduced into airline service:
   A. On Playboy Airlines in the fifties.
   B. After the first incident of passenger airsickness.
   C. During World War II.
   D. In the thirties, by a nurse named Church.

16)   You are a "power flyer" if:

A.   You are a member of three bonus-award programs.

B.   You don't hesitate to write the airlines if you think an employee has stepped out of line.

C.   You make all your preparations in a timely manner to avoid anxiety.

D.   Sometimes, angels with two sets of wings visit you.

17)   U.S. Customs Service:

A.   Pays informers 25% of the amount recovered from any cheating traveler.

B.   Occasionally disrobes people to examine body cavities.

C.   Performs their work enthusiastically in pursuit of truth, justice, and the American way.

D.   Has keys for every type of luggage in the world.

18)   Which perks are available on Air Force One,
      the private jet of the U.S. President, and not
      on commercial airlines?

   A.   Shower.
   B.   Paper shredder.
   C.   King-size bed.
   D.   Shrimp peeler.

19)   The Mile High Club is made up of people
      who:

   A.   At one time or other, have made love
        on a jet.
   B.   Have taken off from Denver Airport.
   C.   Leave magazines under sinks in
        commercial jet lavs, so other mem-
        bers will have something to read in
        there.
   D.   Meditate daily.

20)   "If I had to choose, I would rather have birds
      than airplanes," was said by:

   A.   Charles Lindbergh.
   B.   Amelia Earhart.
   C.   Henry Audubon.
   D.   Juan Trippe.

Part II. Answers to Multiple Choice

1)   B and C are true. A and D are false. B and C are scientific names to define the lack of synchronicity between the environmental (outer) clock and an air traveler's (inner) biological clock. "Cabotage," is when a foreign airline operates domestic flights in another country. Jetlag is caused by changes in light and does indeed affect the brain—possibly resulting in the creation of such spurious answers as "Dimwits' Disease."

2)   A is true. New York/Tokyo takes 13:50 hours. Longer non-stops are San Francisco/Hong Kong (14:00 hours) and Los Angeles/Sydney (14:35 hours). Other double-digit long hauls include Riyadh/New York (12:35) and Johannesburg/ Lisbon (11:35). Although Narita Airport is a few hours by train from Tokyo, it is definitely not the boonies. Rather, it sits in a lovely rural area with charming shops, a temple, and a traffic signal at the main intersection of town which plays music as it changes—a humane innovation for the blind—and the jetlagged!

3)   A, B and C are true. The airlines handpick those whom they seat by exits; these people are projected to be, in an emergency, agile enough to open an exit, and open enough to take directions from a

female (70% of attendants are women). According to airline thinking, this excludes the deaf, blind, handicapped, pregnant, infirm, and obese. Samoans are not obese, but big (nine out of ten require a seatbelt extension). Parents and armed guards are not permitted in the exit rows either—the thinking is they're preoccupied. D is false; Elizabeth Taylor can sit anywhere she wants.

4)   All answers are correct—it's a personal choice.

5)   B, C, and D are true. C applies to domestic U.S. flights; D is international. A is false because two kittens or puppies are allowed per cabin, if they are under ten weeks old; and two birds are always permitted in the same cabin, if they are in the same container. Most 747's have six cabins divided by bulkhead panels: first class, business class, three economy sections, and also one upper deck area which is usually an extra business section.

6)   Only A is correct. Children under two may be held during takeoff/turbulence, or they may sit in an approved child's car seat strapped into a passenger seat. Children sometimes get a 20% discount, depending on routing and never unaccompanied. Children may ride first class, with a discount.

7)   Only D is true.

8)   Only B is true. A is incomplete. C is confused thinking (premature jetlag). D is more or less a homonym.

9)   Only B is counted true for the purpose of this quiz. A could be, if there were only two passengers in first class. First class is often populated with frequent flyers, famous or not, cashing in their mileage awards.

10)   A, B and C are true, excellent reasons to change seats. D isn't; meals are provided according to passenger loads—which doesn't leave a lot of room for the extra-hungry.

11)   A and D are true. Other "acceptables" are calculators, heart pacemakers, hearing aids, shavers, and cassette tape players. Radios are not. One passenger who refused to turn off his radio was convicted of a federal offense. You've got to be careful refusing a flight attendant (on the airplane). B and C are also no-no's. The airlines claim remote devices (including cellular phones) interfere with navigation. However, many experts claim this so-called navigational interference is merely "anecdotal." Some of these

292

experts have posted comments on the Internet at "Healthy Flying" <www.flyana.com>.

12)   C is true. Airlines edit all films, cutting profanity, nudity, politics, religion and, of course, airline crashes. There really was a SAFE Airlines (Southwest Air Fast Express) in 1929; it has since bit the dust. Today there are 1200 airlines worldwide.

13)   A, B and C are true. Perilymph fistula is an inner ear leak which can happen from rapid change in air pressure on descent. Doctors report many passengers catch the flu when traveling. I've seen only three cases of food poisoning. D is false; culture shock can be dizzying, but not normally nauseating.

14)   Only B is true for the purpose of this quiz.

15)   D is true; Ellen Church originated the idea and she was among the original eight stewardesses, all nurses. At that time, other suggested names for stewardess were airette, airess, airmaid, airaide, nidette, courierette, and hostess. The label "flight attendant" began to stick in the seventies when the profession became unisex. Playboy has probably done more damage to the image of stewardesses than any single flight attendant on a bad day.

16)   A, C and D are counted true for the purpose of this quiz. B, on the other hand, is a grumbling flyer, taking advantage of the fact that the airlines dispense disciplinary action rather liberally—adhering to the time-honored belief that "the customer is always right."

17)   All answers are true. Knowing this is smart.

18)   A and B are counted true. The presidential jet, they say, does not have a king-size bed, rather two twin beds, but who knows! MGM Grand Air, which flies between New York and California, boasts a queen-size bed. D is presently classified.

19)   A and D are counted true. There are, in fact, loose organizations (without newsletters) of travelers who've probed the depths of these questions and feel that these are the correct answers.

20)   A is true. Who is Juan Trippe? Juan Trippe was the visionary who birthed Pan Am in 1927, and then proceeded to open commercial air lanes to every corner of the globe. When I worked for Pan Am, passengers would sometimes tell me they were friends of Juan Trippe. If his name did not coin the term "roundtrip," his innovative spirit surely did.

Airmail Stamps

The postage stamps used as illustrations in this text are all from my private collection of air mail stamps. When I was flying, I used to wander into philatelic shops all over the world.

There was one dealer in Osaka, near our layover hotel, who had a lot of nice stamps with airplanes. After a few visits, he asked me, "You live Osaka?"

"No, I'm with Pan Am."

"Ah, so. Pan Am. Very few Pan Am stamps."

My thoughts went immediately to the Pago Pago stamp featuring a Pan Am pontooned clipper sitting in a lagoon, one lone native paddling towards it. I thought of the stamp from the Philippines issued in 1975 commemorating forty years of Pan Am service between San Francisco and Manila. And the 1977 Hungarian stamp featuring our 747 with the distinctive Pan Am round blue logo on its tail.

"Oh, you have Pam Am stamps?" I asked excitedly.

He nodded and crossed the room, opened a large box, pulled out an album, wrong one, pulled out another one. Right one. He half-ran towards me, and proudly placed the open page on the counter. There they were, row and rows of stamps from Panama.

"Panama!" I smiled politely. "I'm not from Panama—I'm with Pan Am," I tried to explain, spreading my arms wide like airplane wings. "You know, Pan Am, the airline." We had a good laugh. And he helped me find more Pan Am stamps including this one from Liberia.

For this edition of JET SMARTER, stamps have been chosen simply from a design point of view—there are no politics involved here. If you have a stamp you think would look good in a future edition, please, by all means, send it to me.

COUNTRY	YEAR/HISTORY	PAGE
Afghanistan	* 1969 * Ariana Airlines airplane flying over Hindukush	320
Antigua	* 1953 * Mail plane over capitol	262
Australia	* 1958 * Super Constellation over the globe, inaugurating Australian round the world service	326
Belgium	* 1946 * DC4 Skymaster Sabena Airlines	340
Benin	* 1977 * Concorde Supersonic Air France	348

Airmail   *Airmail*   *Airmail*   *Airmail*   *Airmail*

COUNTRY	YEAR/HISTORY	PAGE
Nicaragua	* 1931 * Will Rogers and Pan Am	48
Nigeria	* 1942 * Transport Plane	56
Singapore	* 1949 * Postal Union 75 years	38
Switzerland	* 1932 * Geneva Disarmament Conference	130
Tunisia	* 1983 * Woman with Jet Sunglasses	2
USA	* 1954 * Eagle in Flight	122

Thanks to Gordon Medcalf, Hawaiian Islands Stamp and Coin, for dating these stamps.

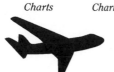

Table of Charts

Endnotes

Why flying is hazardous to your health

1. "New WHO Guidelines on Tuberculosis Transmission on Airplanes," 12/17/98.
2. Meo, Nick, "Rage victim hostess to sue,"PA News, 3/7/99.
3. Repetto, Robert and Sanjay S. Baliga, "Pesticides and the immune system: the public health risks," World Resources Institute, Washington, D.C., 1996.
4. Raloff, J., "Pesticides may challenge human immunity," Science News Vol. 149, 3/9/96.
5. "Cockroach infestation delays Delta flight," CNN.com, 9/19/98.
6. Kay, Jane, "Defending against flying microbes," San Francisco Examiner, 1/30/94.

Jetlag—What causes it?

1. Liese, B, "Medical insurance claims associ-

ated with international business travel," World Bank, Washington, DC, 7/97.

2.   Rayman, M.D., Russell, *Aviation, Space and Environmental Medicine*, Vol. 67, No. 10, 10/96.

3.   Parkins, K.J. et al, "Effect of exposure to 15% on breathing patterns and oxygen saturation in infants: interventional study," British Medical Journal 1998; 316:887-94.

Symptoms & Remedies

1.   Winget, C.M., Ph.D., "Desynchronosis," Navy Aerospace Physiologist Meeting, Flight Stress/Fatigue/Performance Period, 10/16/73.

2.   Raif, S., "Blame jetlag," PA News, 6/11/96.

3.   Brazil track, Sao Paulo, Brazil, AP, 5/23/93.

4.   Baldwin, Alan, "Stallmaier sets pace," Morioka Japan, Reuter, 1/31/93.

5.   Wagstaff, Jeremy, "Karpov, Timman says Chess Duel," Jarkarta, 10/15/93.

6.   Zverina, Ivan, "John Foster Dulles and Jet Lag," UPI News, New York, 3/15/88.

7.   Kilkelly, Ned, "World Trade bombing suspect pleads innocent," UP, 4/4/93.

Time Zones—affecting bodily cycles

1.   Strughold, M.D., Hubertus, *Your Body Clock, Its Significance for the Jet Traveler*, Charles

Scribner's Sons, 1971, p 19.

2. Luce, Gay Gaer, *Body Time, Physiological Rhythms and Social Stress*, Random House, 1971, pp 136-7.

3. Strughold, *Your Body Clock*, p 45.

4. Greist, John H., M.D. and Georgia L., *Fearless Flying*, Nelson-Hall, 1981, p 69.

5. McFarland, Ross, "Air Travel across Time Zones," Aerospace Medicine, 6/74, 45:648.

6. Rachel's Environment & Health Weekly #558, 8/7/97, Environmental Research Foundation, Box 5036, Annapolis, MD 21403, erf@rachel.clark.net.

7. Coleman, Richard M., *Wide Awake at 3:00 A.M.*, W.H. Freeman & Co., 1986, p 69.

8. Wasowicz, Lidia, UPI, "Blame defeat on jet lag," 10/18/95.

9. Cogan, John, M.D., Honolulu cardiologist, telephone conversations and correspondence with permission.

10. Karpilow, Craig, "How the Diabetic Can Best Cope with Jet Lag," The Diabetic Traveler, Stamford, CT, Autumn 1981, p 6.

North/South Flying—magnetic fields

1. Sherson, Robbie, author and retired First Mate, New Zealand Merchant Marines, con-

versations with permission.

2.   Evans, John, *Mind, Body and Electromagnetism*, Element Books Ltd., 1986, p 147.

Mega-Jetlag—an early grave

1.   Ehret, Dr. Charles and Scanlon, Lynne Waller, *Overcoming Jet Lag*, 45:648., Berkley Publishing, New York, 1983, p 149.

2.   "Airline Safety Study of Pilots Older Than 60," AP, Washington, 9/19/90.

3.   McFarland, "Air Travel across Time Zones."

4.   Carruthers, MD, Malcolm, Arguelles, MD, A.E., Mosovich, Abraham, MD, "Man In Transit: Biochemical and Physiological Changes During Intercontinental Flights," *The Lancet*, 5/8/76.

5.   Majendie, Paul, "Heinz 'Bean Baron' Tony O'Reilly, Frenetic Globetrotter," Reuter, Dublin, 10/31/91.

6.   Suplee, Curt, "Eliminating Witnesses; Lawmakers May Aim Questions at TV Screens in the Future," *Washington Post*, 11/7/91.

Compounding jetlag

1.   *Daily Planet Almanac*, 1981, "Jetlag," p 41.

Air Quality—federal prisoners get better

1. Bell, Art, "Coast To Coast AM," Syndicated Live Radio, 2/24/97.

2. Mar, Jacque, M.D., JAMA, 11/20/87, Vol 258, No.19, p 2764.

3. Winget, C.M., Ph.D., and Joan Vernikos Danellis, "Desynchronosis," Environmental Biology Division, Ames Research Center, NASA, 4/16/76, p 8.

4. *Airliner Cabin Environment*, National Research Counsel, National Academy Press, Washington, D.C., 1986, p 196.

5. Spengler, John, Ph.D, Burge, Harriet, Ph.D., "Aircraft Cabin Environment Survey," Department of Environmental Health, Harvard University School of Public Health, 5/21/94, p 1.

6. *Airliner Cabin Environment*, p 7.

7. *Airliner Cabin Environment*, p 156.

8. Merzer, Martin, "Jetliner's recycle cabin air," Knight-Ridder Newspapers, 11/10/94.

9. Phillips, E., "FAA Mandates Lower CO_2," *Aviation Week*, 1/20/97.

10. Trask, Peter, "Aviation Safety And Health," Kitty Hawk, No.2, 11/85, p 1.

11. Bovsun, Mara, UPI Science News, 5/10/98.

12. "Air Travel May Hurt Newborns," Reuters, 3/19/98.

13. McFarland, Ross and J.N. Evans, "Alterations in Dark Adaptation under Reduced Oxygen Tensions," American Journal of Physiology, 1939, 127(1):37-50.

14. "Spoils of success, Corporate America's most powerful people," *Forbes*, 5/19/97, p 204.

15. "Airplane Air," Associated Press, 6/12/96.

16. *Airliner Cabin Environment*, p 43.

Radiation—frequent flyers beware

1. Barish, Robert J., Ph.D., "Business Frequent Flyers—A New Group of Radiation Workers," draft sent to the author on 1/24/97.

2. Barish, Robert J., Ph.D., *Invisible Passenger, The Radiation Risks for People Who Fly*, Advanced Medical Publishing, 1996, p 4.

3. *Airliner Cabin Environment*, p 119.

4. Mims, III, Forrest M., *Science Probe* former editor, e-mail to author.

5. "Not for Primary Screening," *Aviation Week*, 9/2/96, p 10.

6. "Radiation," *Aviation Week*, 6/3/96, p 23.

7. Band, P., Spinelli, J., "Mortality and cancer incidence in a cohort of commercial airline pilots." *Aviation Medicine* 1990; 61: 293-302.

8. Pukkala E., "Incidence of cancer among Finnish airline cabin attendants, 1967-1992," *Brit-*

ish Medical Journal, 9/9/95, pp 649.

9.   Montague, Ph.D., Peter, *Rachel's Environment Weekly* #443, erf@igc.apc.org.

10.   Barish, *Invisible Passenger*, p 5.

11.   *Rachel's Environment Weekly* #443.

12.   Grofman, John W., *Preventing Breast Cancer*, Committee of Nuclear Responsibility, 1995.

13.   Barish, *Invisible Passenger*, p 51-52.

14.   Gridley, Peter, "Radiation Alert: Will Flying Give You Cancer?" *Glamour*, 5/90, p 96.

15.   Orloski, Ray F., Ph.D., Founding Trustee of the Pritikin Institute, "Some Thoughts on Jet Lag," *ARI Newsletter*, no date.

16.   Barish, *In-Flight Radiation*, p 39.

17.   Luxembourg, "The Cosmic Radiation Environment at Air Carrier Flight Altitudes and Possible Associate Health Risks," *Radiation Exposure of Civil Aircrew*, 6/25/91.

18.   Woodman, Peter, PA News, "French to Phase Out Concorde," 3/22/99.

19.   FAA, U.S. Department of Transportation, "Radiation Exposure of Air Carrier Crew Members," AAM-624, 3/5/90.

Ozone

1.   "Adverse Health Effects of Inflight Exposure to Atmospheric Ozone," 7/18/79, Hearing,

Subcommittee on Oversight and Investigations, U.S. House of Representatives, p 11.

2. IBID
3. "Measuring Air Quality" EPA document #EPA451/K-94-001.
4. IBID.
5. Cohen, Carol and Pat Morrissey, "Persistence Results in Ozone Rule," *In-flight Service*, Box 188, Hialeah, Fl, 12/80, p 13.
6. "Adverse Health Effects of Inflight Exposure to Atmospheric Ozone," p 4.
7. Spengler, John, Ph.D., "Aircraft Cabin Environmental Survey."
8. "Concorde threatens ozone layer," Reuters, 2/14/97.
9. Goodwin, Dr. Tony, "Cabin Crew Health Issues," 2/96, http://www.aeronet.co.uk/cspreg.html.

Pesticide

1. Flint, T.N., Regional Agriculture Quarantine Officer, New Zealand Ministry of Agriculture, personal letter to author, 3/29/85.

Toxic Chemicals

1. Rea, William, M.D., *Your Home, Your Health and Well-Being*, Hartley & Marks, p 37.

2.   Baker, Gordon P., M.D., "Aero-Space Workers Syndrome: A disease of our advanced technology," Seattle, WA.

3.   Allergy Hotline, "Flight Attendants Sue Airline Over Illness, Orlando, FL, p 1.

4.   Murphy, Glen, "Ansett sued over fumes on aircraft," sofcom.com, Australia, 3/9/99.

5.   "Smoke in Cabin Forces Evacuation of Continental Jetliner," Newark, AP, 3/7/97.

6.   "Flight Emergency," Fort Wayne, Indiana, Associated Press, 1/15/99.

7.   *Airliner Cabin Environment*, p 30.

8.   Martindale, David, "Cargo Ignites a Controversy," *Frequent Flyer*, 11/88, pp 30-2.

9.   "U.S. cargo company faces charge of pesticide shipping,"" Reuter, Miami, 10/10/97.

10.   "Report Targets Flight Hazards," Associated Press, Cleveland, report by Beth Marchek at *The Plain Dealer*, 1/18/99.

11.   "British Jet Chemicals," AP, 3/15/97.

12.   Galipault, John B., "Airliners and Hazardous Cargo," *Safety Monitor*, Chicago.

13.   Kimball, Rich, "Homegroan," homegroan@aol.com, 7/10/95.

14.   Ashford, Nicholas A. and Miller, Claudia S., *Chemical Exposures; Low Levels and High Stakes*, Van Nostrand Reinhold, 1998.

EMF—electromagnetic fields

1. Lee, Ph.D., Lita, *Radiation Protection Manual*, 3rd Ed., 1990, p 33.
2. Brodeur, Paul, *The New Yorker*, "Annals of Radiation," 6/12/89, p 58.
3. Rea, M.D., William, *Electromagnetic Man, Health & Hazard in the Electrical Environment*, St. Martin's Press, 1989, p 27.
4. Brodeur, "Annals of Radiation," p 85.
5. Edmonds, Sarah, "Swiss Air Shuts Down Entertainment System After Crash," Reuters Toronto, 10/30/98.
6. Barish, *Understanding In-flight Radiation*, p 84.
7. Business Week, 10/30/89.
8. Brodeur, Paul, *Currents of Death*, Simon and Schuster, 1989, p 130.
9. Cook, Wayne and Wanda, *Universal Truths*, 1988, p 67.
10. Lee, *Radiation Protection Manual*, pp 87-88.

High Altitude

1. Werjefelt, Bertil, presentation to Senate Aviation Subcommittee, "The Air That Passengers Breathe," *Frequent Flyer*, 11/85, p 100.
2. Bovsun, Mary, "Air travel can be deadly," UP, 5/10/98.
3. Poppy, J. "Air Travail" *Esquire*, 9/89, p 142.

4.   Kahn, F.S., *The Curse of Icarus*, Routledge, 1990, p 62.

Dehydration

1.   Best, A.S., Pan American World Airways Air Conditioning Tests , Boeing Report No. T6-4453-B747SP, 1976, reprinted in *Aviation, Week*, 2/80, p 170.

2.   Pearce, E.A., *Times Books World Weather Guide*, 1990, p 86.

3.   Kalish, Susan, "Water, the Essential Nutrient," Running & Fitness, Bethesda, MD.

4.   Keates, Nancy, "Water Source," *The Wall Street Journal*, 1/30/97.

5.   Adams, Anne L., "Every Hair in Place," *Frequent Flyer*, 10/91, p 30.

6.   Rippe, James, M.D., PR Newswire, 2/24/89.

7.   Irwin, Michael, M.D., Medical Director United Nations, "Jet Lag Afflicts Many But Few Know The Cure," *Star Bulletin*, 3/20/88.

8.   Xenex Corporation: Aircraft Humidification, "Aircraft-Specific Climate Factors," *Kitty Hawk*, No.13, 1/89, p 2, Honolulu.

Metal Fatigue—when airplanes crack

1.   *Aviation Week*, 2/10/97, p 31.

2.   Tibbits, George, AP Seattle, 3/24/99.

3.   Johnson, Glen, AP Washington, 3/24/99.
4.   Jesdanun, Anick, AP Springfield, 3/24/99.

Airline Policies
1.   Langewiesche, William, "The Lessons of Valujet 592," *The Atlantic Monthly*, 3/98.
2.   "FAA Under the Gun," AP, 6/21/96.
3.   *Consumer Reports*, 1990 Annual Questionnaire, p 465.
4.   *Frequent Flyer*, "Business Travelers," 12/91.
5.   *Fly-Rights*, Civil Aeronautics Board, '82, p 7.

Smoking
1.   PR, Washington, "Petition to Ban Smoking," 7/1/96.
2.   Dow Jones News, "Former Surgeon General Says Seconhand Smoke Causes...," 7/16/97.
3.   Dow Jones News, "Secondhand Smoke Trial," 7/16/97.
4.   AP, Cleveland, "No-Smoking Sentence," 8/18/93.
5.   Mydans, Seth, *The New York Times* reprinted in the *Maui News*, "This is Your Captain Speaking, You Got a Light?" 3/11/90, A5.
6.   IBID
7.   AP, Miami, "Passenger No Smoking," 1/27/97.
8.   Cullen, Joseph W., National Cancer Institute,

"Airplane Study Finds No-Smoking Area No Help," *Honolulu Advertiser*, 2/9/89, A1.

9. Rowan, Roy, "Jetlag Isn't Just a State of Mind," *Fortune*, 4/76.

10. Connor, Michael, Reuter Miami, 7/22/97.

Noise—and pressure affecting ears

1. Goeltz, Judith, *Jet Stress*, Natural Health Sciences, Huntington Beach, CA, 1980, p 31.

2. *Aviation Week*, "Noise Complaints," 4/22/91.

3. Glab, Jim, "Europe's Airport of the Future, Environmental opposition delayed Munich II for three decades," *Frequent Flyer*, 2/92, p 21.

Secure for Takeoff

1. U.S. Federal Aviation Administration, Captain Terry Bowman, Chief, Technology Integration, Secretary of the Air Force, Office of Public Affairs, 3/25/98.

2. Maui News, "The Offbeat: Bad Joke Proves Very Expensive," AP Tokyo, 4/1/91.

3. "Flare Gun—Plane," AP Philadelphia, 1/30/98.

4. Srinivasan, Kalpana, "FAA to Check Security at Airports," AP, 3/11/99.

5. Hahn, Robert W. professor of economics at Carnegie Mellon University, 2/97.

6.   Marshall, Nora C., National Transportation Safety Board, "Passenger Safety Education," *Kitty Hawk*, No. 6, 4/86, p 3.

7.   Borg, Jim, "Nightmare over the Pacific," *Honolulu Star-Bulletin*, 2/26/89, p A-1.

8.   Heftel, Cec, (Member of Congress), letter, *Kitty Hawk*, No.8, 8/86, p 3.

9.   Anonymous, letter to author.

Light Therapy

1.   Robbins, John, *Diet For a New America*, Stillpoint, 1987, p 58.

2.   Winfree, Arthur, "Lighting Up the Body Clock," Shawna Vogel, *Discover*, 1/90.

3.   Czeisler, Dr. Charles, "Jet Lag Breakthrough," *Conde Nast Traveler*, 9/89, p 35.

4.   Irwin, Michael, M.D., Medical Director United Nations, "Jet lag afflicts many but few know the cure," *Star Bulletin*, 3/20/88.

Sleep

1.   "Hazards of Sleepiness," AAA World, 2/94.

2.   Bryant, Samuel, "What Jet Travel Does to Your Metabolic Clock," *Fortune*, 11/63.

3.   "Sweden—Sleepy Pilots," AP, 8/6/95.

4.   Rensberger, Boyce, "Effects of Halcion on Bush," *Washington Post*, 1/9/92.

5.   Reuter, Washington, "Bush Has Stopped Taking Controversial Sleeping Pills," 2/5/92.
6.   Reuter News, Moscow, "Three Days, Four Cities—Yeltsin's Crucial Test," 1/29/92.
7.   Forbes, Mary, "Michelle Honda's Grueling Test," *Flightlog*, Vol.26, No. 2, 1988, p 3.
8.   "Harvard Medical School," 3/88, 13(5), p 8.
9.   Lancet, "Jetlag Pharmacology," 8/86, p 494
10. "Melatonin," PR Newswire, 9/24/97.
11. Arendt, Mary, "Facing Up to Travel," *Frequent Flyer*, 3/91, p 26
12. Winget, C.M., PhD, "Desynchronosis," Ames Research Center, NASA, 4/16/76.

Diet
1.   Ehret, *Overcoming Jet Lag*, p 149.
2.   Houston, Charles S., M.D., "Going High, The Story of Man and Altitude," The American Alpine Club, New York, p 104.

Fearless Flyer
1.   "More than 640M Passengers," AP Washington, 3/24/99.
2.   "FAA probing Chicago plane near-crash on ground," Reuters Chicago, 4/2/99.
3.   *Administrator's Fact Book, FAA,* "50 Busiest Air Traffic Control Towers," 8/91, p 10.

4.   *Aviation Week*, "Assessing Human Factors,"
      12/3/90.
5.   *Aviation Week*, "NTSB Blames DC-9 Crew
      Error for Detroit Runway Collision," 7/1/91.
6.   Coll, Susan Keselenko, "Help for Fearful Fliers,"
      Herald Tribune, 8/7/98.
7.   Magnuson, Ed, "Brace! Brace! Brace!," *TIME*,
      7/31/89, pp12-15.
8.   Bunting, Jane Briggs, "Finding God on Flight
      232," *LIFE*, 9/89, pp 29-32.
9.   McFarland, Ross, "Air Travel across Time
      Zones," 45:648.

Customs

1.   Morrison, Terri, *Kiss, Bow or Shake Hands*,
      Bob Adams, Inc., 1994.

Columns

1.   1996 Gallup Poll, *Your Health*, NY, "Grounding
      your fear of flying," 11/6/96, p 31.

ABC News Columns

The following fourteen questions and answers by Diana Fairechild first appeared as a weekly column in the "Business Travel" section of the ABC News website.

*Just for fun, all the stamps illustrating this section are from
countries that begin with the letters A, B or C.*

Legroom tactics

"Regular coach class seats always make me intensely claustrophobic. What can I do to get one of those roomier exit-row seats?"

The ticket agents assign exit rows. While the agents are checking you in, they're also checking you out. They want someone willing and able to assist in an emergency, so they're looking at your attitude, age, clothes, weight, nationality, fitness and traveling companions. Passengers responsible for others—parents with small children, caretakers with handicapped companions, and armed guards with prisoners—won't be seated in an exit row.

No wimps

The hearing impaired and wimps (some window hatches weigh 65 pounds), won't make it either. Portly passengers (requiring seatbelt extensions) will not be approved because of difficulties they may have maneuvering in the aisles and out the over-wing exits.

On U.S. carriers, English fluency is a must.

Military experience is a plus. High heels are a sore point—they can puncture and deflate an escape chute.

Heavy duties

If you're selected, don't be so comfortable in that exit-row seat that you never get out of it! Mentally rehearse the procedures until you feel confident that you could open the exit door or hatch—because that's exactly what you may need to do.

As the exit row passenger, your first job is to determine if the exit is usable and, if so, to help as many people as possible to get out of that exit. The National Transportation Safety Board cited "passenger inattentiveness" to emergency instructions as a major crash survival problem. The NTSB has also been concerned that "airline passengers have been provided limited, incomplete, confusing and sometimes inaccurate safety information."

Exit rows usually offer more legroom (about three inches), but some can be cold (747's), sometimes the seats don't recline (DC-9's & 737's), and others lack privacy (adjacent to galleys and lavatories). Still, you'll be the first one out in a "water landing."

1. Check in early.
2. Assume a steady gaze.
3. Dress comfortably.

Long flights / fat ankles

"Every time I take a flight, my ankles swell to twice their normal size. What can I do to prevent this, short of hanging upside down from the overhead compartment?"

Hanging passengers upside down might appeal to the airlines. They're always looking for ways to pack more people in—they could call it "vertical class."

At high altitudes, we swell up like the Michelin Tire Man. When a plane reaches cruising altitude, it's at about 35,000 feet and the cabin is pressurized to about 8,000 feet. In this thin cabin air, our bodies expand and, if we don't exercise, our bodily fluids can become stagnant.

The medical term for this pooling of bodily fluids is "dependent edema." It's a bit like what happens with a river—when it's narrow, the water runs swiftly; when it widens, the water moves more slowly and may pool in some spots.

Flight attendants don't get swollen ankles because they are constantly moving, allowing their body fluids to circulate.

Try flexing

Exercise will help. Here are some sets you can do on the aircraft.

1) Squeeze both buttocks together, tightly, deeply, while exhaling, then relax and inhale. In yoga, this is known as *mula bhanda*, a practice that brings vitality. Repeat often.

2) Walk around the aircraft in loping strides with bent knees like Groucho Marx. This will pump more blood up to the brain and is about as aerobic as you can get in a jet. If you bend your knees only slightly, no one will even notice your "Groucho walk," and you will derive great benefit from it. Like the plane, keep moving, adjusting yourself to the changing conditions—the constant bumping and jarring as the aircraft flies.

3) When in your seat, elevate your feet by using your carry-on as a footrest (not during takeoff or landing). Don't sit for too long with one leg crossed over the other; it constricts circulation. Contract, then relax, every muscle in your body.

324

Ginger soothes

One way to reduce swelling in any part of the body is to apply a ginger poultice after landing:

1) Skin and grate a chunk of fresh ginger.

2) Squeeze out excess liquid, then glob the fibrous ginger onto your swollen tissues.

3) Cover with an elastic bandage. (I like to leave it on overnight. It feels hot, but does not burn the skin.)

If swelling bothers you every time you fly, a lifestyle shift may be necessary. Vigorous daily exercise prepares us for physical stress such as jet travel.

Tray table tactics

"The last time I was flying, I desperately needed to work on my laptop. The person in front of me put his seat back, and I couldn't fit the computer on the tray. What should I do next time?"

An economy ticket used to provide a reasonable amount of air space, but every time a plane is redesigned, a smidgen more disappears. Now, what little space remains vanishes into thin air after takeoff as the passenger in front reclines. A "minute to spare" has also vanished for flight attendants, so you may have to handle this situation yourself.

Here's my three-step strategy:

1. Change seats

Go ahead and move to a seat that's behind someone who's not reclining. As long as there are empty seats, you are welcome to take them. Be aware, though, that people next to empties often act territorial—like chickens cooped up in too-small cages, they may peck at you. Regardless, they can only legally save that empty seat if they are holding a second ticket.

2. Shift into business mode—think incentives

If nothing is available, try to swap seats with someone. Offer a drink, maybe, or some travel mileage awards. Travelers from some countries, such as India and Japan, always carry small gifts that might work. Perhaps you could offer a scalp massage—that intruding head is perfectly poised for such an incentive!

Try for a compromise. If you can't get the seat for the entire flight, would you be willing to rent it for a couple of hours?

If you can't relocate, beseech the reclined one in front for just a little more space. Politely explain your dilemma. See if you can trade periods of rest and work.

2. Meditate

Okay, you can get angry—or you can make the best of the situation. Close your eyes. Sometimes creativity trickles in during idle moments. May I suggest that you employ, as well, some motivational thoughts and positive imaging...

> *I feel relaxed. Around us both is a soft white light. I see the intruder bringing his seat to the upright position for the duration of the flight.*

Luggage takes a ride

*"If I check in on the late side, will my luggage be
among the first out of the plane?"*

It's more likely your luggage won't make the
flight at all. On the major carriers, there is no correlation between the time of your check-in and the availability of your luggage.

At the ticket counter, before you say bye-bye
to your bag, make sure it has the correct tag. Read the
three-letter airport code the agent attaches to it, and
verify that it is indeed your destination. Some codes
are easy to recognize: SEA is Seattle. Others are cryp-
tic: BNA (Nashville). Some are tricky: PEK is Beijing.

Once your checked bag is out of your sight, it
is moved, carried and thrown by mechanical means
and by a number of baggage handlers (a.k.a. baggage
mashers)—from belt to cart, to container, to hold, to
cart, to belt.

After landing, the first bag out could end up
under many others piled on a cart, so there's no rhyme
or reason to which bag pops out first at baggage claim—

unless you've got a coveted red "Priority" tag. To get one for your bag, join the airline's premier club, fly first class, or know someone. Your bag will be kept aside, put on last, and rushed to baggage claim.

Sometimes. The airlines admit that when it gets busy, all bags are treated equal. Judge for yourself if it's busy. How full are your flights? When baggage handlers are busy, there's no time for special services—for red tags, soft duffels, or logo luggage—and there are no guarantees of first up at the carousel.

Around the baggage corral we all wait, nervously hoping ours doesn't end up among the statistical eight percent of all checked luggage that gets lost or stolen—or damaged.

Most people don't bother to complain to the airlines about their luggage because the lines at the airport are too long. To be considered for compensation, passengers must file a claim in writing before leaving the airport.

Your best alternative is to travel light and avoid checking luggage in the first place.

Strategies for a quick airport getaway
1. Ship your stuff ahead.
2. Make do with less.
3. Shop as you go.

Coping with queasiness

"When the flight is turbulent, I have to take medication so I don't feel nauseous. Then I'm drugged out for my business meetings. Ear patches don't work for me. Any suggestions?"

Fly the big jets. Avoid smaller commuter planes. Sit near the wing, the most stable place on board. But if turbulence threatens to nauseate, these things help:

1. Breathe deeply.
2. Sip water.
3. Think about other things.
4. Drink ginger root with hot water.

Ginger root is a natural remedy for motion sickness; it's been used against nausea for centuries. I like to skin and grate a chunk of fresh ginger, then bring it on board in a ziplock bag. Add a teaspoon to a cup of hot water (which you can request from a flight attendant), and sip it throughout the flight. You can also find packaged ginger tea at health food stores. Ginger is a natural stimulant. It may continue to help you after you land—at your business meeting.

Lighten the load

Consider flying with an empty stomach. At the aircraft's cruising altitude, the pressurized cabin "interior altitude" is 8,000 feet. This causes our bodies to swell up in all ways. Can you imagine what this does to the intestines and the stomach? An empty stomach, in these conditions, places less stress on the gastrointestinal system. This wards off nausea.

Less internal luggage, less chance of nausea—and fasting when flying helps prevent jetlag.

Think ahead

At the first sign of nausea, scope out an air sickness bag. Some seat pockets don't have any because passengers use them as doggy bags. The airlines don't replenish the seat pockets at every stop, you may have to request one from the passenger next to you or across the aisle. If you have to toss your cookies, use the bag, then close its tabs on the top. If the seatbelt sign is turned off, carry the bag into a lav and dump the contents into a toilet and drop the bag into the trash. Stewardesses are not nurses anymore—not since the early forties. Flight attendants are safety experts and food handlers, so don't hand your "cookies" to one of them.

No predicting rocky rides

"How is it that a plane can hit an air pocket or unexpected turbulence that causes it to suddenly drop over 5,000 feet in seconds? Is there any way to predict this?"

Clear Air Turbulence (CAT), a.k.a. air pockets, is the leading cause of air travel injuries in nonfatal accidents. One of the reasons people get hurt is that the air movements that cause the turbulence are invisible and often unexpected.

While serious run-ins with clear air turbulence are not a routine in-flight feature, they're not rare, either. There are no *clear* statistics about Clear Air Turbulence, but every flight attendant I know, knows at least one person who's been seriously injured in an air pocket.

A variety of conditions can cause turbulence, including changing atmospheric pressure, jet streams, thunderstorms, and cold or warm fronts.

The radar on commercial jets detects only changes in water density (storm-related turbulence), but not changes in wind (air pockets).

Since cockpit radar cannot detect clear air turbulence, we won't hear the pilot warn, "Fasten your seatbelts, folks. It's going to be a bumpy night!"

Buckle up

Current regulations require passengers to buckle up during taxi, takeoff, landing, and whenever the "fasten seatbelt" sign is lit.

Two-thirds of turbulence-related accidents (incidents involving serious injury or aircraft damage) occur at or above 30,000 feet—in other words, when the plane is cruising, not taking off or landing. Therefore, pilots encourage passengers to keep their seatbelts buckled at all times when they're seated.

Child restraints like those used in automobiles save lives when turbulence hits. In severe turbulence, no one can hold on to anything—not even one's own child. About 10,000 small children fly without seatbelts every day on U.S. carriers as "lap children."

Child seats that are 16 inches or less should fit in most coach seats. Parents will then have to buy a seat for the child.

Seatbelts don't protect us from getting battered by bags tumbling from overhead bins. The best way to avoid that is to sit in a window seat and refrain from stashing heavy bags overhead.

Flight attendants' job hazard

Flight attendants are the main victims of turbulence related injuries. In turbulence emergencies, flight attendants must forego their own safety, as their first responsibility is to stow any equipment that could injure passengers.

Only after securing the carts, trays and coffee pots, etc., are flight attendants free to strap themselves in. All this must be done without looking frightened by putting on a brave face for the passengers.

My friend Helen, a flight attendant, was thrown against the ceiling when her plane hit an air pocket. The 300-pound beverage cart also hit the ceiling and then landed on top of her leg. (The food carts weigh less—about 150 pounds fully loaded). Helen had knee surgery, and then she went back to flying.

Hopefully, technology will soon allow us to identify air pockets, so pilots can give advance warning to flight attendants, as well to as parents with infants, in time for everyone to take care in the event of in-flight turbulence.

Fighting jetlag

"My husband and I are taking our first trip to Europe, flying from Boston to Paris. I've been wondering about jetlag. I seem to recall reading something about how melatonin...."

There are dozens of symptoms of jetlag (sleepiness, weak concentration, irritability...) and dozens of remedies that target specific environmental and personal stresses. For example, water is a remedy for dehydration.

During my two decades as an international flight attendant, I discovered and cataloged the more than 200 tips for jetlag that became JET SMART.

The change of environment between Boston and Paris involves shifts in time zones, magnetic fields, climate, culture, and more. En route, the airplane environment deprives us of fresh air and humidity and exposes us to significant amounts of germs, chemical vapors and radiation.

You're also flying east, which means it's harder to get a full night's sleep due to the time shift. The combined effects of all this stress-bombardment are broadly labeled "jetlag."

Columns   Columns   Columns   Columns   Columns

Multitude of woes

Because jetlag is actually a multitude of woes, we can't transcend the whole shebang with a pill. A pill such as melatonin can't fend off all the environmental challenges, and a sedative can exacerbate aspects of jetlag, including fatigue.

Rather than taking melatonin, I prefer to take a hot bath before going to sleep. This is how I managed on hundreds of flights to Europe when I had to get up and work the next day.

Here are three basic preventive strategies for jetlag, which you can apply on any trip:

1) Set your watch to local time before you land.

2) Avoid sleeping on board if your flight lands after dark. Sleep on board only if you land in the morning.

3) Drink lots of water—prior to departure, en route, and for several days after flying. Water relieves many of jetlag's discomforts, including those caused by dehydration, pollution, and altered magnetic fields.

4) Go outdoors. For several days after landing, spend some time in the open air. Even being in a room with windows helps reset the body clock.

338

JET SMARTER by Diana Fairechild

The many effects of jetlag on our global society are stupendous. One billion people fly annually. Certainly everyone on the planet is impacted daily by someone who is jetlagged—for example, someone who nearly runs into you on the highway (impaired coordination is another symptom), or someone who passes the flu to his child, to yours, and by proxy to you.

Jetlag presents challenges to the traveler. All our choices, what we eat and drink, whether we relax and tune in or work relentlessly, can exacerbate or ease our jetlag.

Regarding food, if you can fast on your travel day, that's the best strategy. Then enjoy a meal on local time after landing.

C'est la vie

I love Paris. It was the first place in Europe I visited. The French have a saying, "C'est la vie." (That's life.) If you take long flights across multiple time zones, you'll probably have to deal with jetlag. Yet, jetlag and the environmental stresses en route should no more stop us from traveling than labor stops us from having children. You are on the right track by choosing to be aware of how it will affect you.

Stay open. Have fun. Bon voyage.

Finding room to breathe

"I've noticed the air on planes often seems stale. Is the air better in some parts of the airplane than others?"

Have you ever considered becoming a pilot? The cockpit has ten times more fresh air than the economy cabins. The next best alternative is to upgrade—first class has three times more air than economy. Business class is often stuffy. The curtains in the front and back of this small section impede airflow. The worst place is a coach seat on a crowded flight—more people breathing in a confined space; less air for each passenger.

Scientists have proven that vision is impaired with inadequate oxygen. The airlines, of course, want to ensure that their pilots can see. They won't admit to the connection, though, between oxygen-rich cockpits and pilots' vision. Airline management states that oxygen-rich cockpits are required only for the sake of the aircraft's expensive instruments.

Hypoxia (lack of oxygen to the brain) results in fatigue, inability to concentrate, and a clammy sweat.

In-flight potpourri

What is in the air in airplanes?

Mold, pesticides, toxic chemicals off-gassing from cabin furnishings, germs, viruses, bacteria, spores, lots of carbon dioxide, compounds found in fuels, cleaners, plastic and grease solvents, cosmetics, scents, and more. You can breathe the same things on the ground, but it is more concentrated in jets.

The best place to get fresh air on an airplane is where you sense that you can think clearly and breathe comfortably. No one can give you a specific seat number that will offer you better air, because aircraft configurations (inside seating plans) change, and because some planes fly with leaky seals, broken air conditioners, and dirty filters.

Sometimes you'll find the front of the cabin has more air. For the most part, though, it's where there are the least number of people.

On board, you are free to change seats if you move laterally (business to business) or down (business to economy).

And, it is important to tell an attendant if you experience difficulty breathing. The plane could have a "slow decompression," meaning it is slowly losing air, like a car tire that's always low. It's not something that's going to ground the plane, but it

342

needs to be fixed, so it helps to tell a flight attendant.

You can also ask an attendant to convey to the cockpit that you'd like "full utilization of air." The standard operating procedure on many airlines is to fly with less, but most pilots will turn up the passengers' air when requested.

If you find it difficult to breathe, you can ask for an oxygen bottle. There are about twenty portable bottles (on 747's), and there is no fee in these "emergency situations."

Breathe deeply

After landing, spend time in fresh air—city parks, botanical gardens, by the shore. You can also ask your hotel to provide you with an air purifier and a humidifier.

Oxygen feeds the brain. Shallow breaths coincide with racing thoughts and fear. Deep breaths enhance relaxed, peaceful, creative minds. Fill the abdomen with air, and then let the air rise to the lungs.

The Aviation Clear Air Act of 1996, created to monitor fresh air in commercial jets, was proposed in Congress but never passed. Nor was action ever taken on the 1986 Airliner Cabin Environmental Study which recommended "full utilization of air."

Airlines that continue to treat airplane air as a source for budget-cutting neglect the health of passengers. The more recycled air, the more vulnerable travelers are to the spread of diseases.

Seeking fearless flying

*"....The thing that bothers me most is the feeling
that I've got no control. What can I do to relax?"*

It's a fact. We have no control over the things
that normally cause airplane problems. And, yes, there
are plenty of rational reasons to fear flying.

Some of these demons are news of recent
crashes, the age of many aircraft, the cost-cutting ten-
dencies of airline companies, the effect of sleep deprivation on the crew, the overload experienced by air
traffic controllers, terrorism, bogus parts, and wind
shear.

A recent poll found that 44 percent of Americans dread getting on an airplane.[1] Even Muhammad
Ali, in his heyday, admitted he was afraid to fly.

Here are some tools that may help:

Get Informed

The more you know about the airborne habi-
tat, the more resources you have to draw on to handle

whatever comes up. For example, I believe fear of flying is partially caused by oxygen deprivation, which is an acute and ordinary (but by no means unconquerable) stress for many airline passengers. The emotional reaction of fear, in some cases, is a bodily response to an unhealthy environment.

Take deep breaths. You can even ask for an oxygen bottle on board. I bet you'll start feeling better in 10 minutes.

Get hydrated

The airplane environment is drier than the Arabian Desert or anywhere else in the world. Dehydration affects the kidneys. Weakened kidneys, according to Chinese medicine, cause people to be fearful.

Test-drive this theory: How severe is your fear before and after you drink two glasses of water? Drink a lot of water before, during, and after flying.

Face your fears

Dissect your problem with a desire to discover its mystery. Getting into the nitty gritty will reveal ways out of your problems that you can't imagine until you fully jump in.

So, travel with a notebook and pen, and jot down these facts:

- Note the times of panic attacks and look at their frequency.

- Mentally scan your body. Where do you feel tension? In your head, shoulders, gut, feet? Where is the seat of your fear?

Be prepared

Watch the safety video and review the emergency instruction card. Count the rows from your seat to two exits. Count both forward and aft because a fire in either direction may disable that exit.

Avoid drugs

Use prescription medications only as a last resort. Drugs can throw a jetlagged system further out of whack and cause dangerous side effects.

For those who like shortcuts, here it is: Enjoy yourself. Period. Have fun.

Life is about moving through our fears. We all have to do it whether it's on an airplane, in a meeting, or at the gym. Muhammad Ali had the courage to fly—and so can you.

Buttons call for restraint

"Are flight attendant call buttons for emergencies only? What if I want a magazine? Or a glass of water?"

Flight attendants once had a Pavlovian response to the call buttons. Every time we heard a chime, we would sprint. Not any more—and I blame the aircraft designers.

The old call buttons were overhead next to the reading lights. There, no one ever pulled one without a real need for assistance. But some genius decided to put them in the armrests!

False alarms create chaos

So now, on every flight, dozens of call buttons are mistaken for the recline and light buttons. The buttons are now triggered by pushing in (instead of pulling out), so many of them are set off by errant elbows. The call buttons in the lavs add to the chaos because they are regularly mistaken for flush buttons. This positioning of the call buttons has created an environment in which it's literally impossible for flight attendants to respond quickly to every chime.

Personal attendants are history

The era when flight attendants had the time to leap at every call button disappeared with bell-bottom pants. However, the airlines continue to instruct their marketers to promote the fantasy that any passenger can have a personal attendant at the push of a button—a pretense guaranteed to end in dashed expectations for passengers.

On one flight when I was busy stowing the first-class cabin before takeoff, the life jacket demo tape began to roll at the same moment a call button rang. Regulations required attendants to drop everything while the demo tape rolled, stand by the video screen at the front of the cabin, and watch the passengers. This I did, although simultaneously I scanned the cabin, then nodded when a male passenger signaled he needed help.

When the video was over, I hurried to the gentleman. He looked up at me and said, "I don't feel well," then fell out of his seat face down on the floor. I touched his shoulder, and he didn't move. I called the cockpit, and the captain returned us to the gate. My passenger was carried out on a stretcher.

We heard no more about him.

If everyone only used call buttons for emergencies, the man, who may have died, may have lived.

Pick your moments

I suggest that the call buttons be reserved for passengers who can't get up, or who can't wait. Needing help with small children, for example, is certainly an acceptable reason to ring. Flight attendants won't mind. Most of them have small children of their own.

If your need is not urgent, wait until an attendant approaches your section, gesture for attention and then preface your request with, "When you have time..."

You may find the attendant becomes more attentive. Certainly she or he will appreciate your "jet smarter" awareness of on-board realities. Yes, smart passengers deserve a pat on the back for laying off the chimes.

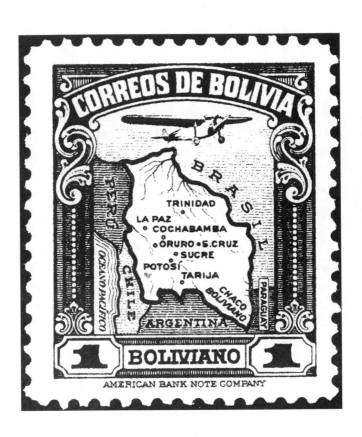

Sipping smart

"What is the best drink to have on the plane? Water, sparkling water, carbonated sodas, or apple juice?"

Apple juice? Once in my life, when I tried a special "liver flush" diet, I actually drank a gallon of apple juice in a matter of hours. It sounds like a lot, but you really should drink about a gallon of fluids on any flight over five hours. Why? Because the cabin air is drier than any desert on the Earth. In radically dry environments, we need to drink much more than we do in the course of a normal day.

Go for a glass an hour

Crew members generally drink a glass of water per hour of flight. I usually drank twice that amount and still experienced symptoms of dehydration, including dry eyes, dry skin, and scratchy throat.

Water is the best drink for combating dehydration. Bottled water is my first choice.

Carbonated or plain? On an empty stomach,

carbonated seems to help balance intestinal gas. In a stomach with food in it, though, I find that carbonation can cause bloating and intestinal distress, as all gases expand at high altitudes. Plain mineral or purified water is most satisfying in the air.

Always bring your own water in case the airplane runs out. Not only can potable supplies dry up, but I've been on long hauls (New York to Tokyo, San Francisco to Hong Kong) where the aircraft actually ran out of all water—even for the lavs.

Some drinks are better on land

Ironically, airline beverage carts promote drinks—such as alcohol, soft drinks, canned juices, coffee and tea—that compound jetlag. Passengers get the false idea that drinking alcohol is a good thing to do while jetting, lured by all those cute miniature booze bottles on the bar cart.

Frequent fliers know that alcohol and altitude do not mix. People get quite drunk in the air, but they don't feel it until they hit the ground like a sack.

Canned vegetable juices usually contain quite a bit of salt, and in flight, excess salt intensifies the "swollen feet and legs syndrome."

It would be another matter if the airlines offered fresh juices, such as carrot-celery juice, which

354

replenishes some of the minerals we lose when we get dehydrated. Orange juice could be a good occasional choice, but it's usually prepared on board, using one part concentrate to three parts tap water.

Consider the source

Here's a tip on the tap water. There are varying standards (and in some cases no standards at all) of cleanliness, treatment procedures and water quality in cities around the world where commercial jets refill. Most airlines have mechanics fill water tanks, as needed, from local commercial aircraft water tanks. Then, to eliminate parasites and bacteria, they add chlorine and bicarbonate of soda to "sanitize and sweeten."

This is yet another reason why I carry my own drinking water.

The airlines also pour coffee and tea liberally at every service. Unfortunately, these beverages, in addition to being made with tap water, have diuretic properties that make the reality of in-flight dehydration even more intense.

Most important, when you fly, be sure to drink a lot of liquids. As we say in Hawaii, "Okole maluna!"—Bottoms up!

#12

Eating right in flight

"What's the best way to get a nutritious meal when you're flying? Are there any foods that should be avoided?"

Would you follow my advice if I told you to avoid all food on airplanes?

Food poisoning is something every airline captain considers on every flight. As a matter of fact, an FAA regulation states that while on duty, the captain and co-pilot cannot eat the same dish. So, when flight attendants say, for example, "Chicken or steak?" captains get their preference, and co-pilots get what's left.

You get what they pay for

Certainly the airlines like us to believe that these meals, which cost them around 70 cents apiece, are nutritious. A trip to the supermarket readily reveals what you can get for 70 cents. But let's look at the basics. I remember the pie charts with four basic food groups that hung in my high school classroom. Meat was in one group and dairy another.

Today, however, both meat and dairy are conspicuously absent from recommended diets for people battling illnesses such as diabetes and cancer. They are also absent from my recommended diet for jetlag recovery.

Carbo loading for altitudes

So then, what is good for fliers? Research on mountain climbers reveals that complex carbohydrates offer a 2,000-foot "altitude advantage"—climbers claim that they function better, even think more clearly, at high altitudes when they avoid high-fat and high-protein foods.

Like mountain climbers, business travelers trying to work in commercial jet cabins, and also after landing, do better on a complex carbohydrate diet.

Complex carbohydrates include grains in their whole form, such as cooked rice, and also in prepared forms, such as pastas and breads. Other complex carbohydrates include just about any "starchy" vegetable.

As a matter of fact, vegetables and fruits are included in all health diets. According to the federal RDA's (Recommended Daily Allowances), you can't eat too much of these two food groups. (And you won't find too much of them in plane fare, either.)

Take out for take off

Since wholesome food is generally not available on jets, I recommend that passengers bring their own. An easy way to do this is to get take-out from vegetarian restaurants, health food stores, and even ethnic restaurants such as Thai, Chinese, and Lebanese.

It's always handy to travel with a plastic or stainless steel food-carrier for packing leftovers. This takes up less space in your carry-on than the styrofoam provided by restaurants.

Abstinence is best

Ultimately, though, I feel it's best not to eat on jets. Picture the physical nature of air travel. The ambient interior altitude of the plane goes from sea level to 8,000 feet in a matter of minutes. This causes every part of our bodies to swell up.

Then, when we land, every part of our bodies contracts. Stomachs and intestines, full of food ingested at high altitudes, carry an extra body burden of gastrointestinal distress. So if you can do it, fasting is your best food selection when flying. Or wait until the captain and co-pilot have digested, and ask them what they recommend!

#13

Flying in style

"I'm wondering what clothing and shoes are best for flight travel as far as safety is concerned. I've heard lots of opinions on the subject, but nothing concrete. Thanks for your answer."

Let's strip away style for a moment and bare the three essentials to be considered when dressing for jet travel:

1) Our bodies always expand in the in-flight, low air pressure.

2) We're subjected to a range of temperatures during flights, and we travel between different climates.

3) There's an outside chance you may need to be dressed for an emergency.

Subtle suiting

There are subtle ways to suit yourself for general health and well-being when you're flying.

Due to the high-altitude environment, our bodies expand after takeoff. I like to wear shoes that are a half-size too big, with cushion inserts. Then, at cruise altitude, I take out the inserts for another perfect fit. Tight shoes can cause serious injury to the delicate veins in your feet. This can lead to swelling and, in the worst cases, blood clots.

Cozy shoes also enable easier movement during emergencies. If you wear high heels, for example, you will be required to leave them before jumping on an escape slide—they can puncture it.

By the way, you'll want to keep your shoes on when you walk around the aircraft, as the floors are often wet (condensation, leaky carts, spills).

Think layers

The air travel experience requires that you endure a wide range of temperatures. Airports and airplanes have hot and cold zones, stuffy and drafty areas. Often, there's a substantial contrast in climate between the land that you depart and the place where you arrive. Layered clothing can be your saving grace.

In case of emergencies

A couple of critical clothing tips for extraordinary circumstances: don't hurt your chances of survival in the event of a cabin fire. While polyester, acetate and nylon clothing will ignite, natural fibers (cotton, wool, silk, hemp, linen) merely smolder, giving you more time to respond and a better chance of survival.

As for crash landings: nylons will cause raspberry burns on your legs if you ever have to slide down one of the aircraft's emergency escape slides. During the early days of training, flight attendants discovered this the hard way.

The "jet smart" dresser is a model passenger on the air travel runway. Go earthy, go layered.

#14

Touchy troubles

"I have heard a few women say that while traveling alone some men started misbehaving— like touching the legs, breasts, etc. Is there a way you can suggest for handling such situations?"

The best course of action is to make the problem known to the purser. The purser is the attendant positioned at the front left door. She or he is the person who makes in-flight announcements. The purser is in charge and has the tools to deal with any problem that might arise in the aircraft passenger cabin.

If the purser is a woman, she may want to get assistance from a male steward or a "deadhead" pilot (a pilot, relocating to pick up or complete an assignment, who is traveling in a passenger seat).

Get out and get help

Rather than confront the offender directly— leave your seat and seek the purser to report your problem. Often the purser will be serving in first class. You can walk up to first class and tell her, "There is a passenger misconduct problem, and I need to report it to the purser."

If you use those words, they'll respond immediately because they realize that you know the insider terms.

When you speak to the purser, give the row and seat number. For example, "The man in 26H is unruly." The purser will then ask you for details, and you can tell her what's going on.

Avoid engaging

If the flight is crowded, she may ask a few people to shift seats. But if you can't move, avoid engaging in conversation.

You can say, "For reasons that are no business of yours, I am uninterested in your advances. If I am further harassed, physically or verbally, I will not hesitate to press charges."

There is no record of the frequency of such violations; most women are too shy to make a fuss. However, it is critically important to hold the offenders accountable for their actions.

Put yourself in the highest light, and others will see and respond to that with appropriate respect.

The Smarter Journey

> ➤ *The following game plan is offered to help remind you of remedies to use on your journey. Of course, you don't need to do everything on this list—but every little bit helps.*

1. Jet Prep: plan, ticket, pack
1) Planning
A. When choosing a flight/airline, consider:
   - -Non-stop vs. multi-stop: *fresh air at stops.*
   - -Flight latitude: *polar flights have more radiation.*
   - -Departure time: *red-eye's cause missed sleep.*
   - -Frequent-flyer awards: *upgrades for miles.*
   - -Price: *deals are available, if you are flexible.*
   - -Departure/arrival time: *travel to/from airports.*
   - -Aircraft types: *wide bodies more comfortable.*

B. Ask Reservations:
   - -Special meal?   -Specific handling?
   - -Wheelchair?   -Supplemental oxygen?
   - -Ask when you are *required* to check-in
     or lose your reservation.
   - -Get "record locator number."

C. Reserve a hotel with these amenities:
   - -Bathtubs.   -Windows that open.

    D. Check with your doctor. Health issues:
- Pregnancy.   -Respiratory illness.
- Cardiovascular.   -Chemical sensitivity.
- Prescribed medication dosage/timing.

2) **Packing**

    A. Clothes. Remember: unscented on airplanes.
- Buy on arrival to accelerate social cycle.
- UNDERpack (less tiring, less expensive).

    B. For warm drink/meal in hotel room:
- Heating coil.   -Transformer/adapter.

    C. Luggage choice:
- Hard luggage less pesticide vulnerable if you check it.

    D. Luggage prep:
- Remove old tags.
- Name/telephone # outside and inside.
- Layover essentials in carry-on in case bag lost.
- Packing list in case bags are lost or stolen.

    E. Packing:
- Double plastic bag anything that might leak.
- Bring drinking water: no cleanliness standards for airline tap water, and most planes don't carry enough bottled water.
- Atomizer to spritz your face with water.
- Sterile cotton for ears.
- Eye-mask.
- Garments—layers plus sweater and socks.

-Hankie: cover nose and mouth.
-Inflatable neck pillow.
-Oil: inside of nostrils and on skin.
-Ultralight cold formula:
   niacin, silk underwear, deep heat lotion.
-Vitamins.
-Herbal tea bags.
-Carbohydrate snacks.
-Zippered jewelry case.
   F. Train for your airport trek: lift luggage.

3) **Body Prep**
   A. Food: plan to fast, OR tote nutritious snacks.
   B. Night before departure: REST!

4) **Subtle Energy**
   A. Visualize yourself en route/at arrival:
      -Happy, healthy, wise, and kind.
   B. Commitment to yourself for entire journey:
      -Careful observation of symptoms.
      -Management of remedies.
   C. Accelerate your social cycle:
      -Travel with others.
      -Be friendly.

5) **Clean up your life**
      -Your business.
      -Your home.
      -Your Last Will and Testament.
            (Not necessarily in that order!)

2. Jet Ready: car/taxi/bus/rail to airport

1) Body Prep

    A. Wake up: -notify cycles change is imminent

    B. No caffeine:

        -Let the novelty of travel stimulate, instead.

        -Arrival cosmology will stimulate your cycles.

    C. Diet: Avoid big meal before boarding.

    D. Bathe: hydrate skin and relax.

    E. Exercise before you go.

    F. Dress:

        -Wear loose clothing: body swells.

        -Covers skin: plane is dirty, dry, pesticided.

        -Natural fiber: less danger in a fire.

        -Rubber-soled shoes: easier to escape.

        -Accessories at the airport: possible upgrade.

        -Accessories for arrival: Customs easier.

        -Suit arrival locale's climate/propriety.

        -Shoe inserts for swelling feet.

    G. Luggage-know your airline's limits.

    H. Call:

        -Radiation!

            Solar flare hotline: 303/497-3235.

            Cancel if proton event.

        -Airport —possible delay/cancellation.

    I. Allow extra time to get to the airport.

2) Subtle Energy

    A. Wear basil sprig/fresh flower for grounding.

3. Jet Set: check-in, security, gate, wait

1) Check-in

A. Seat preference:
- Arrive early, if not preassigned.
- Bring picture ID (even children).
- Window seat: view, privacy, no one climbing over, safer in turbulence (flying objects).
- Less fuel-smell forward of engines.
- At exits—more legroom. Must fit profile.
- Last row—sometimes doesn't recline.

B. Ticket reminders:
- Watch that agent uses proper 3-letter airport code on your bag tag, i.e. NRT = Narita.
- Stow ticket with claim tags and money.

C. Things to request ticket agent:
- Special meal.   -Wheelchair.   -Oxygen.

D. Things NOT to say at the airport:
- Bomb.   -Hijack.   -Gun.

2) Security's X-ray station

A. Keep these from X-radiation:
- Food.   -Photographic film.
- Computer disks.   -Medications

B. Keep your eyes on your personal effects.

3) Wait at gate

- Exercise to prep for hours of sitting.

4) Subtle energy

- Begin tuning into light; sit by a window.

4. Jet Go: enplane, flight, deplane

1) Enplane

A. Board: EITHER as late as possible, due to low oxygen, OR early to get settled.

B. Don't use overhead bin for *very* heavy carry-ons—it could fall and hit someone.

C. Say hello to your flight attendant.
   -If you don't find a pillow and blanket,
      Ask—she or he probably has a stash.
   -Special meal reminder note:
      -Your name.　　　　　　-Your meal.
      -Your seat number.　　　-Your thanks!

D. Tour the aircraft to locate:
   -Possible alternate seat to stretch out.
   -Fire extinguishers.　　-Magazines.
   -Lav locations　　　　　-Alternate exits.

E. Prior to taking your seat, remove:
   -Belt/bulky objects from pockets.
   -Constricting underwear.

F. Emergency: -Count rows to exits.

2) Taxi

A. Fasten seatbelt:
   -Slack, for back and circulation.
   -Outside the blanket, if you sleep.

B. Taxi yourself to sleep:
   -Recline seat as aircraft lifts off runway.
   -Doze off with extra G-force of ascent.

3) **Sleep**
- A. Sleep according to aircraft arrival time:
  - -Avoid sleep on flight if it arrives at night.
  - -Sleep on board if it arrives in the morning.
- B. Cocoon yourself:
  - -Sweater, blanket, eye-mask, ear plugs.
- C. Pillow: inflatable for neck, airline for lumbar.
- D. "Do not disturb" on eye-mask.
- E. Buckle seatbelt *over* your blanket.

4) **Eating on board**. Two options:
- Diet #1: One-Day Fast:
  - -No solid food.   -Gallon water/day.
- Diet #2: Transition Eating:
  - -Eat very light during flight.
  - -Multi vitamin/mineral plus C with meals.
  - -Liquids between meals—float.
- DON'T eat by old/new clocks.
  - (Be guided by what you feel.)
- DON'T adjust to the airline meal service,
  - which is a false social cycle.

5) **Dehydration**
- A. Coping strategy:
  - -Oil nostrils to prevent cracking.
  - -Drink 8 oz. water per hour of travel time.
  - -Request full bottle/can water each service.
  - -Breathe through wet hankie for personal
    humidity and blocking the spread of germs.

-Mist face with atomizer.
B. Avoid alcohol.
  -It's diuretic.
  -You get drunk faster at 8,000 feet.
C. Avoid caffeinated drinks.
  -They're diuretic.
D. Remove contact lenses.

6) **Air quality**
  A. Coping strategy:
    -Ask for "full utilization of air."
    -If it's not enough, ask for an oxygen bottle.
  B. Sudden illness—sore throat, nausea, headache
    -Ask the flight attendant to notify the pilot.
  C. Put rings away because fingers swell.

7) **Lavs**
  A. Wear shoes: The floor is invariably puddled.
  B. Avoid contamination: Wash hands with hot water/soap.

8) **Exercise**
  A. Get out of your seat every hour.
  B. Conscious breathing: to balanced count.
  C. Groucho walk: with bent knees, straight back.
  D. Let body lead: raise arms, pinwheels, etc.

9) **Aisles**
  A. As much as possible, keep feet and elbows out of the aisles, as you could trip someone or get bashed.

10) **If an oxygen mask drops,** pull it to you.

11) **"Air Rage"**

    A. If a passenger is becoming a threat:

        -Act as if you don't notice but leave your seat.

        -Find the purser (in first class).

        -Give the disruptive passenger's row number.

12) **Getting what you want** from flight attendants.

        -Preface your requests with,

           "Please, when you have time....."

        -If there is a selection of entrees, say:

           "I'll have whatever you have the most of."

        -Hot cup of coffee: go to the galley yourself and ask for a "freshly made hot coffee in a paper crew cup."

        -Hot water is always available in the galley for herbal tea or soup if you bring packets.

13) **Subtle energy**

    A. Takeoff: cast off old fears.

    B. Metaphysical athletics: swim, jog, etc.

    C. Aspecting: use clouds to meet subconscious.

    D. Telepathy: connect with others on Earth.

14) **Descent**

    A. Anything inoperative? Tell attendant.

    B. Ears hurt during descent?

        -Yawn, swallow, harden tongue, blow out.

        -"Steam-heat" from attendant (see Ears).

    C. Feeling ill? Request wheelchair.

5. JET DOWN: immigration, customs, baggage

1) Expedite customs clearance

-Accessorize clothing.

-Lean towards agent.

-Sneeze!

-US Customs pays informers 25 percent of the amount recovered from any cheating and also has keys for every type of luggage in the world.

2) Baggage:

-Have claim tags ready.

-Watch out for pushy people with bashing bags.

-Be very careful lugging bags after inactivity.

-Report lost or damaged bags before leaving.

3) What to do while waiting during airport transit stops:

-Aerobic exercise.

-Stroll to the beat of own pulse.

-Stretch.

-Conscious breathing.

-Sightsee.

-Meditate at airport chapel.

4) Airport Services:

Information booth tip: ask for note stating your destination in local language—pin it to your shirt.

5) Subtle Energy:

-Pay attention to inner self orientation.

6. JET LET-GO: car/taxi/bus/rail from airport

1) **Exit airport**

A. Arrival tip: Being met?

If no checked bags,

-Avoid crowds/auto fumes.

-Rendezvous outside Departures.

B. Cold weather formal—

-Niacin.

-Deepheat rub.

-Silk longjohns.

2) Subtle energy

A. Visual grounding:

-Observe shift from old to new world.

-Immerse in light, *as if impressionist painting.*

B. Auditory grounding:

-Hear ambient sounds.

-The unheard sounds.

(Rhythms/speeds of local social cycles.)

C. Touch grounding:

-Embrace family and friends at airport.

D. Scent grounding:

-Inhale scent of local-grown flowers.

-Notice ambient scents.

E. Relax:

-Recall a love felt before.

-Give yourself the gift of that love again.

7. Jetlag: coping with jetlag

1) Water

A. Drink a gallon a day for three days post-flight.
 -To detoxify the body.
 -To rehydrate the body and mind.

B. Submerge in water ASAP!
 -Bath, ocean, pool—whatever is available.
 -A minimum of ten minutes in water.
 -Get your head under water.

C. Therapeutic bath.
   1. Salt/baking soda.
   2. Submerge—even your head.
   3. Drain jetlag.
   4. Cold shower.

2) Diet

A. Eat on local time to reset the time cycle.

B. If fasting while flying:
 -Break fast with watery foods.
 -Soup, fruit, vegetables.
 -Local-grown food accelerates acclimatization.
 -Neutralize radiation with greens—
    (spinach/chard/kale/seaweed).

3) Exercise

A. Stretch: to accelerate adaptability.

B. Aerobics:
 -Tennis/jog/dance/whatever you enjoy most.

C. Nature walks:

     -Provide exercise AND
     -Inform mind AND
     -Orient the cells to local light.

4) **Unpack**
   A. Clean outside of luggage first.
   B. Update your permanent packing checklist.
   C. Store valuables in hotel safe.

5) **Sleep**
   A. Sleep on local time ASAP!
     (If exhausted in the a.m., take short nap only.)
   B. Before sleep:
     -Stretch.
     -Practice conscious breathing.
     -Visualize and affirm.
   C. How to sleep when you're not tired:
     1. Eat your main meal.
     2. Take a hot bath.
     3. Darken the room.
     4. Close the body (eyes, ears).
     5. Split consciousness, then merge it.

6) **Post-flight awareness**
   A. Stepping out in a foreign land:
     -Take hotel name in local language.
       (Matchbook!)
   B. IF YOU:
     1-Catch a respiratory illness within two weeks,
     2-Become seriously ill,

3-Feel that your jet was in poor repair,
THEN YOU SHOULD NOTIFY:
- The Fair Air Coalition.
- Your colleagues.
- Your newspaper.
- Congress.

INCLUDE WITH YOUR NOTIFICATION:
- Flight number/date.
- Aircraft number.
- Sector flown (from/to).
- Date of illness.

7) **Subtle energy**

A. About going to work (Rest first!)
  - After eastbound flights, evenings are best.
  - After flying west, mornings are best.

B. Massage and skin brushing:
  - Restores vitality.
  - Releases endorphins.

C. Tune into:
  - Symptoms.   -Social cycles.
  - Body language.   -Climate.

D. Keep your attitude:
  - Positive.
  - Child-like.
  - REMEMBER, have fun.
      (Time flies when you're having fun.)

Letters

—*J.R., Hazardous Material Container Inspector*
"As a passenger on a 727 on a major airline from Oklahoma City to Philadelphia, I heard this beeping noise. I was kind of joking with my friend about someone's pager going off. Well, after a while of beeping, it turned out that it was *my* Oxygen Indicator sounding its alarm. The oxygen meter I carry lets me know if the oxygen level drops below 19.5 percent, which is supposed to be the borderline of sustaining human life. Personal indications of oxygen deficiency are dizziness, light-headedness, and goofy feelings. During the whole flight of three hours, my meter sounded its alarm; the only way we have of turning it off is to get out of the hazardous environment."

—*Rochelle Rabin, Esq.*
"Thank you for your work against spraying on airplanes. How could the airlines authorize spraying poison on people? It's just nuts."

—*N.H.*
"I am a law clerk with a small law firm. We represent a man who had severe sinusitis when he boarded an airplane. (He was not warned against this by his doctor.) The pressure in the cabin so severely hurt him that he went to a hospital upon arrival. It was later discovered that his sinus membrane had burst, leaking fluids into his brain, causing a brain infection. I am currently researching possible causes of action in this case. I would greatly appreciate any help."

—*John Duffy*
"My travel has resulted in a number of rather serious illnesses. In just the last two years, I contracted the chicken pox (I'm 38, with no kids, and no known contact with children for at least 30 days before contracting the disease), two severe sinus infections, and food poisoning. Each of these appeared to be the direct result of an international air flight. The food poisoning was eight hours into a flight on an established carrier from N.Y. to South Africa."

—*Dr. Lucy Miller*
"Your book really helped to change my own travel strategies. I just returned from a round-the-world journey in the middle of flu season without a problem."

—*Evelyn Staus*

"I flew roundtrip from Minneapolis to Nairobi. All the flights on the way over were relatively miserable, but the return flights were almost unbearable. At one point, I felt so ill from the cabin air that I thought I might lose consciousness. Of all the miseries involved in long distance air travel, cabin air quality—or lack thereof—is by far the worst problem. If you are doing anything of an organizational nature to work for clean air in airplane cabins, I would be interested in getting involved."

—*Karen Meyer*

"I slept on the airplane during the flight, and woke up as we were making our descent. I then experienced rapid onset of extreme nausea, lightheadedness, tingling/numbness in extremities and face, ears ringing, and I nearly blacked out. I thought I was having a stroke."

—*Martin T. Cresdee*

"I noticed I was having to 'pop' my ears quite frequently. About 20 minutes after landing, I began to have a nauseous headache. The pain was over the bridge of my nose. I eventually got to sleep and when I awoke, I had had a nosebleed in my sleep. The cabin pressurization must have burst a blood vessel."

—*Gareth Morrell*
"I recently contracted flu which led to pneumonia in the middle of a hectic series of flights, so I will now try to pluck up my courage and ask for more oxygen as you suggest.

—*John Strong*
"I, like two million other Americans, suffer from lung disease. I was stunned by your information. I pay a ridiculous price for supplemental oxygen and jump through all of the hoops in order to get it when I fly. Many other sufferers could not do this, so they have to travel without the benefit of additional oxygen, depending upon what they believe to be good air in the plane. This is really criminal."

—*M. Ferrin*
"Thank you for the tips on keeping my nose moist on long flights. While growing up I had a friend who got frequent nose bleeds, but the only time my nose ever bled was when I was hit in the face with a soccer ball—until I spent 20 hours on a flight that took me from Dallas to Chicago to New York to Buenos Aires to Santiago, Chile. Somewhere between New York and Buenos Aires, my nose started to bleed. Since I never had nose bleeds, I knew it had to be from the cabin air. Thanks for the tips!"

Author's Biography

The toxic conditions on airplanes caused international flight attendant Diana Fairechild to lose her health. After 21 years and 10 million miles of flying, she was "medically grounded" and diagnosed with "toxic chemical poisoning." Symptoms of chemical poisoning are similar to Gulf War Syndrome and Sick Building Syndrome.

Fairechild is now an airline passenger advocate, alerting travelers to the health dangers of flying. From her home in Hawaii, she writes and, when she can, counsels people about safe air travel, fear of flying, and healing from chemical poisoning (detoxification) with Hawaiian herbs.

Fairechild has been quoted in hundreds of media sources including *Forbes*, *USA Today*, *Whole Earth Review*, *Dateline* (about pesticides in jets), *MSNBC.COM* (about airport security), *CNN* and *Hard Copy* (recycled air), *Bridal Guide* (honeymoon travel),

Houston Chronicle (fear of flying), *Philadelphia Inquirer* (dehydration), *Los Angeles Times* (seatbelts), *Family Life* (flying with kids), *Meetings in the West* (abusive passengers), *Delicious* (healthy skin when flying), *Marie Claire* and *Glamour* (jetlag), *Business Week* (indoor air pollution), and *Washington Post* (athletes' jetlag).

A number of magazines, newspapers and web sites have featured Fairechild as an expert in aviation health and safety including ABC News, CNN and Reuters News Service.

"Healthy Flying with Diana Fairechild" on the Internet <www.flyana.com> has been called one of the twelve most creative web sites by *The New York Times*, and it was reviewed by *TIME*. The site has developed into a worldwide forum for airline passengers to network and lobby for improved health and safety conditions.

People sometimes want to know why the site is called "flyana." In Fairechild's own words:

Flyana is a nickname from my flying years and because it rhymes with Diana, I like it. Rhyming makes me laugh. Diana Flyana reminds me of "Saturday Night Live's" feature Rosanna Bombanna. I also like the word flyana because I'm attracted to all things that fly, especially airplanes, birds, and dragonflies. Further, I'm single because I'm waiting for Icarus to fall out of the sky right on to my front porch.

How Toxins Affect Us

The following narrative, entitled "Understanding Chemical Sensitivities," was written in 1991 by James M. Miller, M.D. and presented as part of Diana Fairechild's legal challenge to United Airlines following the denial of her Workers' Compensation claim for chemical poisoning in her workplace.

Humans, like all living creatures, are by nature biochemical organisms. Our continued good health is dependent upon the proper functioning of innumerable enzymes participating in an enormous number of biochemical reactions.

These reactions must take place at the proper time, at the proper rate, to the proper extent.

We see, smell, taste, hear, balance, walk, talk, chew, swallow, reproduce, sleep, think, and remember as a result of the proper functioning and proper balance of the many biochemical processes that support these functions.

Chemicals enter our bodies through the skin, the gastrointestinal tract, and the respiratory tract. Certain substances are useful to the body and support its biochemical mechanisms, while others are not useful or are even harmful. The latter are called xenobiotics. We exercise relatively little ability to be selective and tend to take in some of all the chemical substances presented whether they are desirable or not.

Once in the body, chemicals are distributed by the blood to all organs. Chemical substances, which are not inert, have the capacity to combine with the chemical substances of the tissues, forming new compounds and altering the function of the tissue elements with which they have combined.

A xenobiotic that combines with an enzyme will alter the function of that enzyme. As a result, the chemical reaction dependent upon that enzyme may become too slow, ineffective, or perhaps not take place at all. This would result in a deficiency of some essential substance or an accumulation of some intermediate substance, both of which are harmful to the coordinated, balanced, physical/chemical mechanisms of the body. Xenobiotics can combine with and alter the function of any tissue component in the body, i.e., cell membranes, proteins, as well as enzymes.

We are fortunate in that we are endowed with excess capacity in all our organ systems. We have two kidneys, but can survive on the functional capacity of one normal kidney. We have two lungs, but can survive on just one.

The capacity of most of our enzymes and biochemical processes is greater than we usually require. Because of the excess capacity in all our organ systems, we are able to sustain considerable injury and diminution in functional capacity before there is any organ malfunction and, therefore, any symptoms.

Xenobiotic chemicals do their damage to our body's chemical mechanisms one molecule at a time. Individuals exposed to xenobiotic chemicals on a regular basis will experience regular injuries that will accumulate over time to eventually result in organ malfunction.

Whether or not one develops illness from chemicals depends upon the extent of the injury caused by any given exposure, the rate at which the injury can be repaired, and the frequency with which the exposure and the injury are repeated.

If one goes to work and sustains an eight-hour exposure to a solvent, some of the solvent will enter the body and combine with some of the tissue components, causing a finite amount of injury.

This is true even though the level of the solvent exposure may never have exceeded the OSHA standard or any other standard that might be considered "safe." If the injury can be completely healed in the sixteen off duty hours, the individual returns to work at 100% capacity and the situation is sustainable indefinitely. If the extent of the injury is greater than can be repaired in the off duty hours, the individual returns to work at less than 100% capacity.

This sequence of events will be repeated each work day, and the individual will accumulate injuries, injuries which will eventually lead to erosion of the excess functional capacity and organ malfunction. This process will remain unnoticed until the loss of functional capacity results in symptoms. At this point, the slightest increase in this dose of the xenobiotic in question will provoke symptoms each and every time it is encountered.

There is a period of time when the injury is occurring, but the excess capacity has not yet been eroded away, so there are no symptoms. There is another period where the extent of the damage results in symptoms, but the individual can still sustain life and might recover if the exposure were to be terminated, although not necessarily without residual damage.

There is the final period where organ damage is irreversible and incompatible with life. This sequence pertains to exposures to chemicals, such as cyanide, solvents, pesticides and any other chemical capable of entering the body.

Sensitivity to a chemical results when the previous exposures to that chemical and/or other xenobiotics have caused sufficient cumulative injury that the excess functional capacity has been eroded away. At this point, a chemical exposure that appeared to be well tolerated previously is no longer tolerated, and is now encroaching on vital capacity.

It is a common observation that individuals who become sensitive to one chemical often begin to react to others. This is because the body has a limited number of detoxification mechanisms. When the mechanism has been damaged, all chemicals that are eliminated through that mechanism will not be well handled and will provoke symptoms.

Individuals vary greatly in their abilities to resist the damaging effects of chemicals. It is always the individuals with the least capacity to tolerate chemicals who are the first to become sick. Others in the group might tolerate the same chemical exposure indefinitely without apparent illness.

Nobody in the world today is free from some degree of chemical body burden. Individual tolerances and exposures may vary greatly, but we are all somewhere on the spectrum between minimal burden and having taken on that last bit of chemical that pushes us over the brink into a state of chronic illness.

JAMES M. MILLER, M.D.
BINGHAMTON, NEW YORK

Fair Air Coalition

Diana Fairechild, founder
PO Box 248, Anahola Hawaii 96703–USA

The Fair Air Coalition is a tax-exempt, non-profit, charitable support and advocacy organization run by airline passengers for the benefit of airline passengers. It focuses on education and research into health problems induced by air travel. The Fair Air Coalition is involved in:

- Focusing media attention on aviation health issues.

- Educating legislators and the public on maladies induced by flying.

- Understanding flight-related health problems through research.

- Collecting testimony which provides evidence relating illness and aircraft toxicity.

Many of the conditions that impair passengers' health are preventable. The airline must be brought to recognize that passenger health is an important issue and that passengers are no longer willing to accept poor or dangerous environments.

There is turbulence ahead, but this is not the time to remain seated.

In 1997, two Scottish television executives caught a drug-resistant strain of tuberculosis on a commercial airline, according to their producer who interviewed Diana Fairechild. How many airline flights are so dangerous? The airlines' common denial of the risks exacerbated by their equipment and practices is a sore point of contention for passengers who become ill, even with a simple cold or flu.

But for those with serious medical conditions, the experience can have deadly consequences. While it is known that deaths have occurred during flights, there is no data on the exact numbers. (The airlines aren't telling.) In addition, some passengers who become ill on board, die after landing.

Doctors are now warning people with the following medical conditions to be cautious when flying or not fly at all: pregnancy, epilepsy, emphysema, asthma, mental illness, heart disease, recent strokes.

To become a member of the Fair Air Coalition, send a donation in any amount, or call (800) 524-8477 to donate by MasterCard or Visa. The Fair Air Coalition's activities are supported by donations.

Speaking Engagements

Arrange for Diana Fairechild to speak to your group in Hawaii, or bring Diana to your conference or business anywhere in the world. Diana's enthusiasm for her topics is inspiring.

"Board members will not want to board another plane until they've heard what Diana Fairechild has to say."—*American Board of Trial Advocates*

For easy to follow, engaging presentations, call 800/ 524-8477. Topics include (among others):

A. "Master Jet Travel"

"Thanks for the informative and occasionally shocking information we all need when we fly. Your candor and humor are priceless."—*J.R. Reinking*

- Get better air quality on flights: avoid the flu and other on-board infections.
- Employ coping strategies for in-flight environmental toxins: pesticides, fuel exhaust and radiation.

- Have special needs met: tall passengers, wide bodies, specific diets.
- Pack smart. Dress for comfort, safety, and potential upgrade.
- Fall asleep easily in an airplane seat.
- Overcome fear of flying.

B. "Detoxification"

"Diana Fairechild has done more to raise awareness of environmental toxins than anyone we know."—*Environ magazine*

- Detoxification using the ancient herb, noni.
- Avoidance therapy at home/work.
- Rotation diet/recipes.
- Mental restoration and new neural pathways.
- Heat and ocean detoxification.
- Intravenous vitamin C.

C. "Publishing Coach"

"Diana did magic. She took a hick from Kansas and helped free his pen to soar high on the winds of creativity."—*Mike Farmer, commodities broker*

- Organizing your manuscript.
- Book design, copyright, Library of Congress.
- Agents, foreign rights, distributors.
- How to get free publicity.
- Marketing on the Internet.

Ordering

Write, phone, fax or e-mail. For contact information, please turn the back page. Your personal checks, Visa, MasterCard and Amex are welcome.

Please remember to add shipping-handling. Below each item are two s/h charges, such as $4/$6. The first is for airmail in North America; the second for airmail anywhere else in the world. Thank you.

JET SMARTER: The Air Traveler's R_x

Is flying dangerous to your health? Yes! Even if you're only an occasional flyer, this book can minimize the dangers and ease the discomforts of air travel. Flying is not what it used to be. Today, commercial jets have inadequate and toxic air. "Thanks, Diana. You're doing great work, and I refer many people to your book. All are amazed (and grateful) for its contents."– David Stenn, screenwriter

Autographed copies $14.95 s/h=$4/$6

Fearless Flyer Consulting

Are you afraid to fly? Diana Fairechild has developed an unusual and very successful technique to aid fearful flyers. Fearless Flyer will transform your fears—with warmth, with humor, and with simple, powerful strategies, including brainstorming and positive imaging. You are not alone. You can be cured.

"Your advice to trust was very helpful. I actually, for the first time ever, looked out the window upon takeoff."—Pam Finamore

"I have much to look forward to going to Europe soon. Love awaits me there if I have the courage to go get it. May God help me, and I thank Him for putting you on my path."—Pedro E. Lecusay

For help with your fear of flying, e-mail <diana@flyana.com> or call <808/ 828-1919> for consultation rates and availability.

Two Diodes for protection from radiation

Diodes are made from 47 different elements, each carrying its own electrical frequency, creating a protective, electromagnetic field around the body. Diana wears two diodes at the computer and when flying.

Each diode measures one-inch square and is 1/4-inch thick.

$44 for two + s/h=$4/$6

398

NONI: Aspirin of the Ancients.

Fairechild's book on noni (an ancient herb) is filled with stories of pain relief and healing from myriad illnesses—arthritis, cancer, diabetes, Epstein Barr, hypertension, poisoning, and more. Our immune systems are compromised daily by the air we breathe and the food we eat—so it is reassuring to find one food, noni, which can actually reverse the effects of toxins. "Fairechild is an authentic visionary and a gifted writer, and her latest book is a wonderful example to the healing spirit she brings to all her work."—Jonathan Kirsch, attorney/author/book reviewer, Los Angeles

Autographed copies $9.95 s/h=$4/$6

OFFICE YOGA: A quickie guide to staying balanced and fit in the work environment.

Prevent and eliminate painful headaches, carpal tunnel syndrome, and back aches caused by sitting for long hours at the computer. Here are effective yoga postures you can do at work in your office clothes and in just a couple of minutes. These 20 easy yoga postures with illustrations are from Diana Fairechild's own therapeutic practice. Fairechild has practiced yoga for 36 years.

Autographed copies $9.95 s/h=$4/$6

for more information

contact: Diana Fairechild

Box 248 Anahola, Hawaii 96703—USA

fax : 808/ 828 - 1313

Phone: 808/ 828-1919
Ordering line: 800/ 524-8477
Orders from abroad: 808/ 639-9900
E-mail: diana@flyana.com

"Healthy Flying" on the Internet
the JET SMARTER companion website
www.flyana.com/

books

consulting

presentations